HELP! I'm a Parent
Christian Parenting in the Real World

10 Interactive Programs
for Parents of Children Birth to Age Seven

Drs. Claudio and Pamela Consuegra

Authors: Drs. Claudio and Pamela Consuegra
Editor: Kathy Sowards
Design & Layout: Liv Jacobson
Project Manager: Brad Forbes

Project Committee:
Dr. Claudio Consuegra
Dr. Pamela Consuegra
Brad Forbes
Wilma Kirk-Lee
Karen Pearson

Special thanks to the subscribers to Adventist Parenting e-newsletter for sharing your parenting challenges, concerns and ideas on what subjects would be most helpful in a parenting resource.

Additional copies available from:
Advent*Source*
5120 Prescott Avenue
Lincoln, NE 68506
www.adventsource.org

Printed in the United States of America

ISBN# 978-1-57756-034-0

TABLE OF CONTENTS

MEET THE AUTHORS

Drs. Claudio and Pamela Consuegra currently serve as the Family Ministry Directors for the North American Division of the Seventh-day Adventist Church. The North American Division territory includes the United States, Canada, Bermuda, and the Federated Islands of Micronesia.

Claudio was born in Colombia, South America, while Pamela grew up in the Appalachian Mountains of Virginia. They have been married for more than 30 years.

Claudio has served as pastor in various conferences throughout the United States. He has also been a law-enforcement, hospital, and hospice chaplain, a marriage and family counselor, and conference departmental director and administrator. He holds a Doctor of Ministry degree in Family Ministries from Andrews University.

Pamela has a background in Adventist education, having served as a teacher, academy principal, and Superintendent of Schools. She holds a PhD in Leadership from Andrews University.

Claudio and Pamela have a rich background in the area of family ministries having worked as a husband and wife ministry team throughout North America. They have served in numerous conferences, hosted a live call-in family show for LifeTalk radio, and authored numerous journal articles as well as several books.

They have two adult daughters: Diana, an English teacher at Takoma Adventist Academy, and Hadassah, a Doctor of Osteopathic Medicine, and a son-in-law, Greggory, who works as a Speech and Language Pathologist.

Claudio and Pamela are passionate about building strong, healthy marriages and families for God's Kingdom. They believe strongly that this process begins in the home as parents partner with God on the most rewarding task in which they will ever participate—parenting!

DEDICATION PAGE

This parenting manual is dedicated with love to our two girls, Diana and Hadassah.

Our greatest privilege in life is having been invited by God to co-parent with Him and raise our two daughters for His glory.

Drs. Claudio and Pamela Consuegra

FOREWORD

In a national survey of the state of families in America (Bowman, 2012), parents reportedly believe that raising children today is more complicated than it used to be. Along with that, most perceived that the quality of American family life was declining. In addition, 55% of the parents surveyed expressed a concern that they were not doing a very good job of parenting.

In essence, the study concluded that "for today's mothers and fathers, there is no clear map that charts the path for nurturing the next generation of adults" (Bowman, 2012, p. 10). We bring you good news. There is a map! And this map that charts the path of parenting for you is the Word of God. The principles of parenting in scripture are timeless.

In a survey conducted by the North American Division Department of Family Ministries, parents of children from birth to age seven were asked to identify their biggest parenting challenges. Each of the topics discussed in this resource is a response to the needs expressed by those parents.

The purpose of this resource, *Help! I'm a Parent: Christian Parenting in the Real World*, is to inspire and encourage you on your journey to be the disciple-makers of your children. You will be motivated to take up the exciting challenge and experience the blessings of parenthood.

We realize that one resource will not answer all of your parenting questions. Therefore, we have set up a website to accompany this resource. Please visit us at ***www.HelpImAParent.org***. There, you will find additional resources and materials that will add to your discussion on each of the topics. In addition, you may submit questions, sign up for a parenting newsletter, subscribe to a parenting blog, and much more.

We invite you to journey with us as we explore your God-given role of parenting. May you be blessed as you take on one of life's most rewarding tasks of raising your child to be a disciple of Jesus Christ.

Drs. Claudio and Pamela Consuegra
Family Ministries Directors for the North American Division of the Seventh-day Adventist Church

REFERENCES

Bowman, Carl D. (2012). Culture of American families: A national survey. Institute for Advanced Studies in Culture. Charlottesville, VA: University of Virginia.

HOW TO USE THIS RESOURCE

I. COMPONENTS

This parenting resource consists of three main components:

1. **Manual**—"Help! I'm a Parent: Christian Parenting in the Real World" Manual

2. **DVD Set**—These that contain a 30-minute segment that accompanies each of the chapters in the manual.

3. **Website**—This is a very important component of this resource. You will find additional resources posted on each topic. You will also be able to submit any unanswered questions that you may have, sign up for an e-newsletter, and follow a parenting blog. The website will be updated on a regular basis, and serves as the place to go to keep this information current and relevant. The website is ***www.HelpImAParent.org***

II. WAYS THIS RESOURCE MAY BE USED

There are three ways to use this resource:

1. **With a Group**—It is recommended that you use this resource in a group setting. Perhaps you can do it in your church and invite all the parents in your congregation to join you. You might invite all your neighbors to your house to participate in this parenting enrichment program. It is a great way to meet felt needs as well as get to know your neighbors better. You may choose to facilitate, or a facilitator may be designated to lead in the group discussions and activities. You do not need to be an "expert" to lead out in this program. You only need to be open to group processes and be willing to let God lead you.

2. **As a Couple**—You may proceed at your own pace and share your ideas with your partner. If there is an opportunity, invite at least one other couple to join you in the experience. You will all benefit by sharing varying views, experiences, and insights.

3. **By Yourself**—It is possible to do this program by yourself. However, why not check around and invite at least one other person to join you.

III. SESSION FORMAT

1. The first session should follow this format:

   a. Greet each participant as they arrive.

   b. Have opening prayer as soon as all the participants have arrived.

   c. Share a light meal or a snack.

   d. Have participants introduce themselves and share a little about their family. They only need to share as they are comfortable to do so.

   e. Distribute the manuals.

f. Assign participants the homework of reading over chapter one and be prepared to discuss it the next time you meet. Suggest that group members work through the activities and come prepared with any questions they may have at the next meeting. It is not expected that they will answer every discussion question, complete every activity, or understand every concept discussed. The group will work together next week; you only want them to become familiar with the material in the chapter beforehand.

g. Announce the day and time for the next meeting, where chapter one will be introduced. If you wish, you may let the group members help you decide. You want to be sure it is a time to which they can can all commit. The dynamics of each group will be different, so be as flexible as you can.

h. End with prayer.

i. You may want to check with each participant a day or two before the scheduled meeting as a reminder.

Note: The purpose of this first get together is to get acquainted with each person, to start to build community, pass out the manuals, and give the assignment to read chapter one. You will not be discussing chapter one in this session. It is a meet and greet session.

2. Each successive session should follow the same format:

a. Begin with prayer.

b. Review scriptural principle.

c. Go over the Icebreaker/Group Discussion Questions with the group.

d. Together, watch the 30-minute companion DVD that goes with the chapter to be covered in that session.

e. Lead out in the chapter discussion. Review each topic. Lead out in the group discussion questions and activities. The participants only need to share as they are comfortable in doing so.

f. If participants have any questions discuss them as a group.

g. Remember to remind the participants at every meeting to visit the companion website for additional materials and resources.

h. Assign the next chapter for group members to read.

i. Announce the day and time for the next session.

j. End with prayer.

Note: If you find that you need more than one session for each chapter, that is not a problem. You make it work for your particular group's needs. If needed, you may take several weeks or sessions for each chapter.

IV. KEY SECTIONS IN MANUAL

This manual is divided into ten chapters. Each chapter addresses a topic that was identified by you, as parents, as one of your biggest parenting challenges. You will find these elements included in each chapter of the manual:

1. **Scriptural Principle**—Each of the ten chapters is guided by a spiritual principal that opens the chapter.

2. **Icebreaker/Group Discussion**—The purpose of this activity is to encourage discussion of the scriptural principal for the chapter. This section will ask you to remember, review, and reflect on what the passage teaches.

3. **Group Activity**—This section is activity-based. You will be asked to write responses to the question presented. In some cases you may do this as an entire group. In other instances you may be asked to do this individually and then share your responses with the entire group.

4. **Group Discussion**—This section will either contain a question for the group's consideration or a statement on which to read and reflect. You are to process it together with your group members.

5. **Sidebars**—Please take time to read all the sidebars. They each contain valuable information that adds to the current topic of discussion.

6. **Try This at Home**—This section will challenge you to try certain activities at home. You do not have to attempt all of them at once. However, we do encourage you to select one idea and try it as you complete each chapter.

7. **A Prayer You May Say**—This is a suggested prayer for you to pray. Of course, you may say one of your own.

Above all, enjoy the parenting journey. It is our prayer that as you learn together, find answers together, pray together, encourage each other, and grow together in the task of parenting, you will be blessed and enriched.

1. INVITATION AND INTRODUCTION: CHALLENGES OF CHRISTIAN PARENTING IN THE REAL WORLD AND INVITATION TO JOURNEY WITH US

SCRIPTURAL PRINCIPLE

"And these words which I command you today shall be in your heart. You shall teach them diligently to your children, and shall talk of them when you sit in your house, when you walk by the way, when you lie down, and when you rise up. You shall bind them as a sign on your hand, and they shall be as frontlets between your eyes. You shall write them on the doorposts of your house and on your gates" (Deuteronomy 6:6-9).

ICEBREAKER—GROUP DISCUSSION

1. REMEMBER
- Share one of your fondest childhood memories of your family. What made that event so special to you?

- Do you remember any valuable lessons you learned as a child from an adult—from your parents, grandparents, or another significant adult? How did they impress that lesson upon you (a story, a conversation, a saying, modeling, etc.)?

2. REVIEW
- Read Deuteronomy 6:1-9. For whom were these words of Moses intended?

- Why do you think there's such emphasis on the teaching of laws, beliefs, and principles?

3. REFLECT
- How do you demonstrate your love for God? How does that fulfill verse five? What can you do today to demonstrate it? What can you do to teach your children to show God their love?

- How important is it to you that your children grow up to love God and appreciate His presence in their lives? How can you help teach them about God's love?

OVERVIEW

Have you, as a parent, ever felt like screaming out for help? The reality is that Christian parenting in the real world of today can be challenging. This resource is a response to cries for help. It was developed as the result of a survey of parents throughout the North American Division territory, including the United States, Canada, Bermuda, and the Micronesian islands. Respondents were asked to identify their most challenging areas of parenting in today's world. The topics covered in this series are a response to those felt needs. This chapter serves as a basic overview of the biggest challenges that parents face today. Subsequent chapters will then take these challenges one by one and deal with each separately.

From managing busy schedules to dealing with outside influences, parents have their hands full these days. There is broad agreement among the public that it is harder to be a parent today than it was in the 1970s or 1980s. A national survey by the Pew Research Center (2013) finds a widespread belief that today's parents are not measuring up to the standard that parents set a generation ago. Mothers are seen as having the more difficult job, but they are also judged more harshly than are fathers. More than half of Americans (56%) say that mothers are doing a worse job today than mothers did 20 or 30 years ago. By comparison, somewhat fewer people (47%) say fathers are doing a worse job than fathers did 20 or 30 years ago.

The biggest challenge in raising children today, according to parents and non-parents alike, is dealing with the outside influences of society. Some of the specific challenges identified by parents and addressed in this manual include:

- Changing Picture of Home: How do we build a firm foundation?

- Secularization of Society: How do we help our child turn from the secular to the sacred?

- Me First: How do you teach your child the importance of sharing and service?

- Healthy Relationships: How do you deal with sibling rivalry and help your child build healthy relationships?

- Media: How do you deal with the invasion of media in everyday life?

- Health: How do you help your child incorporate healthy principles into their life choices?

"Parents, are you working with unflagging energy in behalf of your children? The God of heaven marks your solicitude, your earnest work, your constant watchfulness. He hears your prayers. With patience and tenderness train your children for the Lord. All heaven is interested in your work . . . God will unite with you, crowning your efforts with success" (White, 1952, p. 205).

- Discipline: How do you teach your child to be respectful and responsible?

- Too Little Time and Too Much Stuff: How do you teach your child to manage their time, talents and treasures?

- Lack of Support System: Where and to whom can you go when you need help with your parenting challenges?

CHANGING PICTURE OF HOME

As soon as a young child has the motor skills to hold a crayon, one of the first pictures they will draw is a picture of their family. These are the individuals that the child recognizes as significant in their upbringing. I can still remember drawing that picture of my family in kindergarten. In fact, I ran out of room on my paper as I tried to draw my mother, father, two brothers, one sister, and all four of my grandparents. And, of course, I wanted to include all of my aunts, uncles, and cousins. I saw all of them as "family." Indeed, they all lived in very close proximity to me and our home was their home. At the same time, every aunt and uncle shared the role of parenting us with our mother and father.

However, today's picture that the child draws may look different. Living close to one's large extended family is not as common as it used to be. The North American society today is very mobile. Instead of living next door to your relatives, you may live across the country. A short walk away or a short car ride away daily or weekly has now been replaced by a plane trip once a year or two. As a result, the number of significant adults in the lives of some children is shrinking and the number of adults who share in the parenting responsibilities are becoming fewer and fewer. We no longer enjoy the broad social support system families once did.

In addition to seeing a decrease in the number of extended family members living close by, we also have evidence that the number of homes with a single parent raising a child has significantly increased. A study entitled, "The State of our Unions" (2012) found that as recently as the 1980s, only 13% of the children of moderately educated mothers were born outside of marriage. By the late 2000s, this figure rose to a striking 44%.

Another trend in today's world has been the increase of grandparents raising their grandchildren. Current studies reveal that in the last 10 years, the number of children living with their grandparents has increased by 50% (Livingston, 2013).

As a result, when a child is asked to draw his/her family picture today it may be that of the grandparents with the child, a mother and child, a single dad, adoptive parents with their biological parent in another house, a child with two moms, a child with two dads, or a foster child may draw several homes with varied family make-ups. And these are but a few of the variety of scenarios they may picture.

As the household make-up differs from the past, so do the challenges of parenting. No two homes are exactly alike. No matter what your home may look like, the reality is that no home is challenge-free. Yes, all of those entrusted with raising a child experience both the joys and challenges that come with home life. We all have those days when we shout, "Help! I'm a parent!" The good news is, although the picture of today's typical family may differ somewhat, God is the same yesterday and today! And He, our Heavenly Parent, loves us and is eager to help us build our homes on a firm, healthy, lasting foundation.

SECULARIZATION OF SOCIETY TODAY

Many parents today blame society, in general, for their biggest parenting challenges. Recently the results were released on the largest study ever conducted on families in America (Culture of American Families, 2012). Less than a quarter of today's parents agree that this is a great time to be bringing children into the world and most say it is tougher to raise children today than it was 50 years ago. This view is accompanied by a generally gloomy assessment of the family's trajectory in American society. The study found the following:

· Among other things, nearly half (49%) of parents agree that "in general, Americans lived more moral and ethical lives 50 years ago" than they do today; those who disagree with that assessment are in the minority (only 24%).

· Less than 1 parent in 10 (8%) thinks the quality of American family life has improved since when they were growing up.

· 64% say that family life has declined.

What is more, the decline in the family is part of a larger view of the decline in America: Parents who think the family has declined also see a decline in our nation's educational opportunities, the quality of American schools, the safety of American communities, the quality of the popular media, the strength of the American economy, and many other things. Eighty percent of those who say there has been a "strong decline" in the family also perceive a "strong decline" in American moral and ethical standards overall. They believe that the "honesty and integrity of the average American" has waned. The perception of family decline is part of a larger perception that our communities are less safe, our work ethic has slipped, and American religious and spiritual life has ebbed. In other words, parents believe that the family structure is in decline because America is in decline.

So, what's a parent to do? Do you throw up your hands and admit defeat as you look at the decline and secularization of society in which you live? If you believe the same thing as the parents in the above survey, then this belief should actually motivate you to action! That should be your wake-up call to be more intentional about raising your child, to focus less on the secular and more on the sacred. You must be intentional about building a strong spiritual foundation in your home. Values such as honesty, integrity, and a strong work ethic must be instilled in your children. Our homes and family life can reflect Jesus to our secular communities. Even though the world may have different values, your home can fly the banner of Jesus Christ. One home and one child at a time can impact your world for Jesus! We will look at ways to help you turn your child's eyes away from the things of this world and upward towards heaven.

GROUP ACTIVITY

1. What values would you like your children to learn? Make a list. Why are those values important to you? Do you live by those values?

2. What have you observed in the society today that conflicts with the principles and values you would like your children to learn? Give specific examples.

ME FIRST

An additional area that concerns today's parents is the "child-centered" society. There seems to be more of a focus on what "I need" instead of looking at and responding to the needs of others. In other words, the world of today is described as a "Me First" society. Athletes raise their hands and shout, "I'm number one!" Frank Sinatra sang, "I did it my way." And, before committing to something it is common to ask, "What's in it for me?"

"Bible promises are pain killers and life savers" (Kuzma, 2006. p. 35).

Do you find it challenging to teach your child the opposite of this self-centeredness that they are exposed to? After all, teaching young children to practice the golden rule and put others first takes time. Service and community-related projects just seem to be one more thing that needs to be scheduled. Perhaps some things have to be eliminated from the family's calendar and service activities need to be intentionally added. Doing so will prove beneficial to the receiver and to your family.

Yes, teaching your child to share and to put others before themselves takes time and effort. At the same time, perhaps you are making it too hard on yourselves. Small things can oftentimes make a difference in the lives of others and at the same time teach your children big lessons of selfless service. We will explore ways to teach your child to be open to the needs around them and to have a servant's heart.

HEALTHY RELATIONSHIPS

If you have more than one child, chances are that you have already encountered sibling rivalry. Teaching them to get along with brother or sister is one of your first parenting challenges. A battlefield can emerge in the back seat of your car, in your living room, or in the children's bedroom. In fact, where two or more of your children are gathered, there will most likely be a fight! Does this describe your home?

Another challenge is teaching your children to get along with their peers outside the home. Even if you only have one child, this could be an issue for you. This may mean getting along with relatives, other children in the daycare facility, children at church, or other friends or neighbors.

"God not only created you; he created your children. And he chose to place those children in your home. To doubt any of this amounts to nothing less than questioning the sovereignty of God" (Thomas, 2005, p. 13).

Good relational skills in toddlers build the foundation for healthy relationships later in childhood and throughout adulthood. Don't despair. With God's help, coupled with prayer, patience and persistence, your child will develop positive relational skills. We will look at ways to help you deal with sibling rivalry and turn your home from a battlefield into a peaceful haven. We will also explore ways to help you guide your child in building healthy relationships outside the home environment.

SOCIAL MEDIA

Arguably one of the biggest challenges of parenting today is dealing with the onslaught of media. It comes at you and your child from every direction. As soon as you have one gadget mastered, another comes on the market.

Do you often feel as though you are constantly competing with media as you strive to teach values and morals to your child? The struggle becomes all the more difficult when television sitcoms portray children being disrespectful to their parents, as if it were "normal" and "no big deal." What was unacceptable behavior yesterday has become "normal" and even expected today. In numerous ways, the media condones the very behaviors you are trying to eliminate from your home.

The over-use and abuse of media has changed the way entire families communicate. Look around you the next time you go with your family to a restaurant. How many people do you see texting or talking on their cell phones, playing on their iPad, listening to their iPods, or playing with some other electronic gadget? Chances are good that you will see this all around you.

Interaction with media has replaced meaningful dinnertime conversation. Instead of sitting down as a family at the dinner table, more and more families are hastily gobbling down their food while sitting in front of the television or the computer monitor. It is not at all uncommon for each family member to be scattered all over the house in different rooms, engaged in various forms of media entertainment. Readily available media prevents families from sitting down and talking with one another on a heart to heart level at the dinner table.

But let's be honest and make this real. It is all too easy to use various forms of media as a "babysitter." It works and it's free. Your child is occupied and quiet. They even have their favorite DVDs from a very early age or watch them online from their own tablet. And even the tiniest child can be taught how to touch an iPad, access their apps, and play their games. The colorful and moving graphics are appealing to them and keep their interest in ways that nothing else seems to do.

The truth is that media is a great babysitter if all you want a babysitter to do is keep your child quiet and allow you to do what you want or need to do. At the same time, however, the ultimate cost is too great.

Take a media inventory in your home. How much time are you as a parent consumed by it? How much time is your child engaged in various forms of media use? Start now and commit this challenge to prayer—that God will reveal to you, as a parent, areas where change is needed in your family life. We will take on this challenging topic and learn practical ways of managing media in your home.

QUESTIONS?
As you begin this study, make a list of the challenges you face as a parent today. Cross them off as they are addressed in this resource. If they are not addressed, please contact us so we may address them or post additional resources on our website. You may also submit questions directly on our website at **www.HelpImAParent.org**

GROUP ACTIVITY

1. Individually make a list of all the electronic gadgets you had as a child. Make a list of all the gadgets your children have. Which ones do they use or spend the most time with? Share your responses with the entire group.

2. Did you have any electronic gadgets when you were growing up? What gadgets does your child have (computer, iPad, television, etc.)? Where is it? In their room? Do they have free access to these things or is access restricted? Do you monitor the use?

HEALTH

Another area that parents highlighted as a concern was in the arena of health. Teaching children the importance of making healthy food choices and getting a proper amount of exercise is too often neglected. Health also includes teaching your child habits of good hygiene and having an awareness of your child's mental health status.

Here is another area where we see the availability and use of electronic gadgets helping account for children's lack of exercise. When I was a child, I was always outside playing ball, riding bikes, playing hide-and-seek, or catching fireflies. Inside was boring! Today's children have television sets, video games, computers, and many more electronic gadgets in their rooms. And all too often, young children are left unsupervised in their use of these devices. Why go outside and exercise? Being a couch potato and watching television or playing on the iPad is so much more fun. Unfortunately, this lack of physical activity is showing up in higher obesity rates and more social isolation in children.

Teaching healthy food choices can be challenging as well. In fact, it is easier for today's parents to pop that sugar-frosted pop-tart in the toaster for breakfast, warm that frozen meal in the microwave for lunch, tear open that bag of chips as a snack, hand over that store-bought cookie, and stop at a fast food place on the way home from daycare or school. The preparation of healthy food takes time, thought, and effort and adds one more thing to do!

Healthy habits, however, can become a lifestyle for the whole family to practice together. Things such a family walks, meal planning, and cooking together can become enjoyable family experiences. Together we will explore how healthy living is a lifestyle that the entire family can benefit from and have fun doing at the same time.

GROUP ACTIVITY

1. What health concerns do you have for your family? Are these concerns rooted in health problems with your family of origin?

2. Make a list of good, healthy practices you already have in your home.

DISCIPLINE

What is the definition of punishment? What is discipline? Is there a difference? How can you teach your child to be self-governing and to make choices not because you say so, but because it is the right thing to do?

Some parents state that their day seems consumed with settling disputes. Who wants to hear arguing all the time? Who wants to scream at their child over and over again to get them to do anything? Respect seems to have gone out of the door for many children today. Parents claim that their real job is more like that of a full-time referee.

In addition to being respectful to each other, all members of the family should have some responsibility for a well-ordered home. How young should this start? What are appropriate expectations? Teaching your child to be respectful and responsible is worth the effort, but it takes consistency. We will look at the answers to all of these questions and discover ways to help your child be both respectful and responsible.

TOO LITTLE TIME AND TOO MUCH STUFF

Too little time is one of the biggest challenges for parents. Twenty-four hours a day is not enough time. Modern society puts so much emphasis on productivity and activity. If you could just slow down, think of the win-win situations you could create not only for your children, but also for your entire family.

Think about this for a moment. When do most of the daily power struggles occur in your home? When your preschooler is dawdling over putting his shoes on and you're running late? Or when they want to stay on the playground but you have to leave so you can make dinner, supervise homework, get baths, have devotionals, pack lunches, and are still in bed on time? The time crunch is truly a pressure cooker that makes it challenging for you, as a parent, to live in the moment and just enjoy your child.

Parents often feel torn between professional and parenting responsibilities. When focusing on one, you may feel like you are neglecting the other! This is a common dilemma for today's parents, who often have schedules packed with innumerable tasks and responsibilities. How do you balance work and family responsibilities when both seem pressing?

GROUP DISCUSSION

Calculate the following:

1. How many hours in one year?

2. How many hours do you and your children spend in church in one year?

3. How many hours do your children spend at school?

4. How many hours do your children spend sleeping and eating?

Once you have calculated each of these, add #s 2, 3, and 4 and subtract them from #1.

Now consider the following questions:

1. Considering the number of hours your children spend at school, church, and with you. Who has or should have the greatest influence in their life?

2. Are you depending on the school or the church to disciple your children? Or are you partnering with the school and church to help you with that task?

3. Of all the hours you have with your children, how are you spending them? Watching TV? In extra-curricular activities (sports, music lessons, etc.)?

Talented children abound today. This must be the case because we as parents have them signed up and involved in every imaginable activity. They go to soccer practice, dance class, art class, yoga class, swimming lessons, etc. Yes, you need to recognize and encourage the talents that you see in your child. But could you be overloading them? Are there better ways of encouraging them to develop and use their talents to bless others?

Today's families have too little time, too much to do, and too much stuff! Instead of learning to be creative or value what they already have, children who are constantly showered with toys and gadgetry merely master the first commandment of out-of-control consumer culture: Stuff equals happiness. What does your child treasure? Are they valuing material things over heavenly treasures? Does your child equate stuff with happiness? Would your children rather have more toys or enjoy more quality time with you?

When we consider the whole realm of teaching our children to be good stewards of their time, their talents, and their treasures, are there areas where *we* need to improve? Are we teaching them to manage all of these things so that they will glorify God? We will explore ways to teach your child to be good managers of their time, their talents, and their treasures.

LACK OF SUPPORT SYSTEMS
Rather than the village raising the child, parenting has become something we do isolated within the walls of our homes. Keep in mind the statistics shared at the beginning of this chapter. As the make-up of our families has changed, so have our support systems.

Where can you go as a parent on those days when you feel overwhelmed? Who can partner with you on the most important task you will ever undertake? How do you know when you need more guidance than mom, a friend, or a pastor can offer? We will look at ways of partnering with others as you take on the awesome task of parenting your child.

WRAP UP
With all of the challenges of today, parents may be tempted to throw up their hands and accept defeat. Regardless of the make-up in your home, it is important to remind yourself that God has called you to parent your child " . . . for such a time as this" (Esther 4:14). In other words, regardless of the circumstances in which you find yourself, whether a grandparent raising your grandchild, a single parent, a foster mom, a couple, etc., God has called you at this time and for His purpose. And when God calls, He also enables. Do not despair. God is bigger than any of the parenting challenges this world can throw at you.

In subsequent chapters we will take each of these challenges, one at a time, and explore it in depth. We will look at each challenge through the principles that are given to us in God's word. We will consider current research and break it down into practical parenting principles that we can apply in our homes. And most of all, we will lean on our Heavenly Parent for wisdom and guidance. We invite you to continue with us on our journey of learning to be a Christian parent in the real world of today.

GROUP DISCUSSION

1. Discuss the statement below. How may it be applied to Christian parenting in today's real world? What does this offer as something you can do to help your parenting role? What will be the result?

"Parents may well inquire, 'Who is sufficient for these things?' God alone is their sufficiency, and if they leave Him out of the question, seeking not His aid and counsel, hopeless indeed is their task. But by prayer, by study of the Bible, and by earnest zeal on their part, they may succeed nobly in this important duty, and be repaid a hundredfold for all their time and care . . . The source of wisdom is open, from which they may draw all necessary knowledge in this direction" (White, 1954, p. 64).

GROUP ACTIVITY

List what you consider to be the biggest challenges of parents today:

TRY THIS AT HOME

1. Throughout this course we will encourage you to engage in a "Bible Promise Project." That will start today. Find a promise in the Bible that speaks to you, as a parent, about overcoming the challenges of parenting in the real world of today. Write it out on an index card and put it in a prominent place in your home throughout this week. Place it where you can see it throughout the day. Repeat it often, memorize it, and claim it as your own. And remember to share it the next time you meet with your group members.

2. Pray daily and commit yourself to God as a Christian parent. If you are married, pray with your spouse. If you are not married, find another single parent to partner with. If they are not currently in this study group, invite them to participate in these lessons with you.

3. Ask God to guide you in the specific parenting challenges that you face. Lay yourself before Him. Remember, however great the challenges—He is greater still!

A PRAYER YOU MAY SAY

Dear Lord, the challenges of parenting today are great. But the good news is that You are greater. I pray for wisdom as I parent my child. I want to dedicate myself and my child to You. Help me to be faithful to this God-given responsibility. Show me where I need to change. Above all, help me to reflect You to my child. In Jesus' name, Amen.

REFERENCES

Institute for Advanced Studies in Culture. (2012). *Culture of American Families: Executive Report.* Charlottesville, VA: University of Virginia.

Kuzma, K, (2008). *The First 7 Years.* Nampa, ID: Pacific Press Publishing.

Livingston, G. (2013). "At Grandmother's house we stay." Retrieved from http://www.pewsocialtrends.org/2013/09/04/at-grandmothers-house-we-stay/

National Marriage Project. (2012). *State of our Unions.* Charlottesville, VA: University of Virginia.

Pew Research Center. (2013). "Motherhood Today: Tougher Challenges, Less Success." Washington, D.C. Retrieved from http://www.people-press.org/2007/05/02/motherhood-today-tougher-challenges-less-success/

Thomas, G. (2005). *Devotions for Sacred Parenting.* Grand Rapids, MI: Zondervan.

White, E. G. (1954). *Child Guidance.* Washington, DC: Review and Herald Publishing Association.

White, E. G. (1952). *The Adventist Home.* Hagerstown, MD: Review and Herald Publishing Association.

HELP! I'M A PARENT WEBSITE

Visit our parenting website to submit questions, find additional resources, follow a blog, sign up for a free parenting e-newsletter, and more: *www.HelpImAParent.org*

2. FIRM FOUNDATION

SCRIPTURAL PRINCIPLE

"For which of you, intending to build a tower, does not sit down first and count the cost, whether he has enough to finish it—lest, after he has laid the foundation, and is not able to finish, all who see it begin to mock him, saying, 'This man began to build and was not able to finish?'" (Luke 14:28-30).

ICEBREAKER—GROUP DISCUSSION

1. REMEMBER
· Was there ever a time you took risks you now wish you hadn't?

· If you were on a TV game show, and you had already won some money, would you risk losing it and take the chance to win even more? Why?

2. REVIEW
· As you consider the Bible verses of our spiritual principle, what kingdom values does Jesus teach in the entire section (Luke 14:25-34)?

3. REFLECT
· When did you realize that following Jesus was costly? How so?

· Have you ever stopped to consider since then if the cost was worth it? What keeps you going?

OVERVIEW

Every builder will tell you that the most important component in a stable building is the foundation. It doesn't matter what the rest of the building looks like if the foundation is not solid. Andrew Morison (2011) reminds us that the foundation of our homes is indeed the most critical part of the construction process. Any mistakes made in the foundation get worse as you go higher up in the construction process. Even the untrained eye will clearly see defects as the building gets higher and higher.

Think about this same concept and apply it to parenting. The same way in which a foundation needs to be strong for a good building, we need to have a firm foundation when it comes to parenting our children. If not, just as a building will reveal defects as it goes higher due to a weak foundation, the "defects" will clearly be seen as our children grow if our family foundations are not firmly grounded in strong Biblical principles.

As we consider making sure we have a firm foundation for parenting we will look at the following:

· Preparation for Parenting
· Unexpected Arrival
· Marriage Matters
· Personal Spiritual Growth

GROUP ACTIVITY

Complete this activity individually and then share your response with your group members. As you embark on this journey of being the type of parent that God has called you to be, perhaps you need to reflect on your personal parenting goals. How would you finish this sentence . . .

As a parent, I want my child to be the . . .

smartest?

fastest?

prettiest?

most popular?

richest?

What is your ultimate parenting goal? You must know what your target is before you can aim for it.

PREPARATION FOR PARENTING

Read our scriptural principle for this chapter again, "For which of you, intending to build a tower, does not sit down first and count the cost, whether he has enough to finish it—lest, after he has laid the foundation, and is not able to finish, all who see it begin to mock him, saying, 'This man began to build and was not able to finish?'" (Luke 14:28-30). What does it have to do with parenting? This verse reminds us of the planning that one does before a building is constructed. Notice that planning takes place prior to construction. One must first consider the materials needed and the cost to complete the project. This takes a great deal of thought and careful preparation.

When it comes to parenting your child, what planning took place prior to your child's arrival? Was any preparation required? You may have set up the baby's room with a crib and stocked up on diapers, T-shirts, and baby pajamas. But what did you do to prepare in other, more important ways? The truth is that we plan and prepare better for most other things in life. As a teenager we take driver's education in order to get our driver's license. We go to college and get an education for our chosen career path. And, in order to maintain required certifications, we even go to continuing education classes. We may even enroll in cooking classes or art classes in order to develop our hobby. But when it comes to parenting, we usually assume this role with little or no preparation at all.

"Children are the heritage of the Lord . . . " (White, 1952, p. 159).

In the ideal situation, preparation would have taken place before even becoming pregnant. However, with so many unplanned pregnancies today, parenting preparation is usually the exception to the rule. There are many things to consider before taking on the parenting role. If, however, you are already a parent, don't despair. It is not too late to think about these things.

1. Spiritual Readiness—You will be co-parenting with God. Have you committed yourself completely to Him? Are you ready to listen to Him? (Refer to "Personal Spiritual Growth" section that follows.)

2. Financial Preparedness—Are you financially secure to add a baby to the household? Babies require a great deal of financial resources to provide for their many needs (diapers, formula, clothes, health care, education, etc.).

3. Your Knowledge in Child Development—Are you familiar with the growth and development of a child? Do you know the stages of sexual development? Are you aware of age-appropriate behavior at varying stages of growth? (See the additional materials provided at the end of this chapter.)

4. Sibling Preparation—What if you already have one child and desire another? Your child should also be prepared for the arrival of little brother or sister. What are some things you can do to make an addition to the family an easier transition for them?

5. Unity in Parenting—Whether you are married or single, there should be unity among all parties who are actively involved in raising your child. Before the baby arrives, discuss things such as church attendance, discipline, education, health practices, etc. When it comes to child rearing, there needs to be unity— everyone needs to be on the same page.

GROUP DISCUSSION

How do you think Jesus would have parented?

UNEXPECTED ARRIVAL

With birth control so readily available, it may surprise you to know the statistics as they relate to unplanned pregnancies. The Guttmacher Institute of Washington D.C. reported that about half (49%) of the 6.7 million pregnancies in the United States each year are unintended (September 2013). This is a startling statistic. The fact that about one half of all babies born today are not planned definitely brings some challenges. How can one plan for something that is not expected? Is it any wonder that the foundation may not be laid when no building was ever planned?

The reasons for unplanned pregnancies may be innumerable. Perhaps it was a missed birth control pill, a woman caught in mid-life crisis, or a teenager who got carried away in the heat of passion and made a poor choice to engage in pre-marital sex. In such cases, one may be forced to delay education, postpone that sought-after degree, turn down a job promotion, or move back into the home with Mom and Dad in order to care for the baby.

Others find themselves functioning in the role as a parent, and yet they are not the biological parents. Such is the case of grandparents today. More and more grandparents find themselves serving as the primary caregiver for their grandchildren (Livingston, 2013). Perhaps they had thought they were finished with child rearing and ready to enjoy their retirement years. However, circumstances have dictated that they raise their grandchild. They, too, may have to undertake the unexpected duties of parenting.

GROUP DISCUSSION

Unexpected Arrival as a Grandparent, Foster Parent, or Adoptive Parent

Unexpected circumstances may force relatives to become parents. One such situation is the accidental death of a biological parent. The child may be taken into a foster home or adopted by an aunt, uncle, or grandparent. Another unexpected situation can develop when adult children hand the custodial right of their children to their own parents. Reflect on the following questions:

1. How do these unexpected changes affect the dynamics of the adoptive, foster family, or grandparent's home?

2. What challenges does the child experience? If you have biological children in the home, what challenges do they face as additional children join the family?

MARRIAGE MATTERS

If you are married, how does becoming a parent affect your marital relationship? Perhaps it is no surprise that Kari Adamsons (2013) discovered that, on average, couple relationship quality declines following the birth of a first child. After all, a new baby demands a great deal of time—time that used to be reserved for each other is now focused on baby. Any precious time that is left over is dedicated to much needed sleep.

Why is it that research reveals a decline in marital satisfaction after a baby arrives? "For many couples, the experience of becoming a parent can undercut or diminish the quality of married life. This is partly because parenthood is stressful and partly because children often limit their parents' one-on-one couple time. Spouses with children at home reported spending nearly two hours less per day together than did those without children at home. Thus, couple time might be particularly beneficial to couples with children at home, in so far as it is more of a precious commodity for these couples" (Wilcox & Drew, 2012, pp. 9).

Just as a new baby requires time and attention in order to grow, so does your marital relationship. The challenge is in finding time. So, we ask, how much time does it take to make a difference? The Date Night Opportunity (2012) finds that "couples who devote time specifically to one another at least once a week are markedly more likely to enjoy high-quality relationships and lower divorce rates, compared to couples who do not devote much couple time to one another" (Wilcox & Drew 2012, p. 14). This means that as little as one intentional date a week can make a significant difference in your marriage relationship.

"When our kids see how we deal with failure, disappointment, frustration, and our own limitations, they are learning. Are we building a secure refuge, or will it be a shoddy cardboard house that won't make it through a single storm? Do they witness a faith that will last through cancer, unemployment, frustration, and stress, or are they looking at a belief that wilts under the slightest spiritual assault?"
(Thomas, 2005, p. 16)

In addition to nurturing the relationship with your husband or wife, time together will also benefit your child. "On average, children who grow up with two married parents enjoy higher living standards, better health and better developmental outcomes than children in other types of families. These children also tend to advance farther in school, behave better, abuse fewer substances and achieve more success as adults, spouses and parents" (Ribar, 2004, p. 24).

Time nurturing the marriage relationship is time well spent. It creates a win-win situation for you as a couple and for your child.

The best gift that you can give your child is not the latest and newest gadget. It is not more "stuff." Rather, the best gift you can give your child is the gift of a good marriage. This creates a sense of security for your child. Nurture your marital relationship. Do not feel guilty about spending quality time with your spouse. In doing so, you will be strengthening the very foundation that your home is built on.

PERSONAL SPIRITUAL GROWTH
The most important relationship that needs to be nurtured in the home is the relationship each family member has with Jesus. Whether you are a married or single parent, an adoptive or foster parent or a grandparent, we all need to have a personal relationship with Jesus. A firm foundation in the home begins with the foundation laid by each individual family member. Each individual's spiritual health will combine to form the overall foundation.

If you have a newborn baby, you know that it seems as if every moment is consumed with caring for Baby. And at the end of the day, you just want to collapse in bed before the baby cries and awakes you for the next feeding. How do you find quiet time alone to sit and commune with Jesus? Perhaps you can think about spending time with Jesus all throughout your day. For example, even if you are changing your baby's diaper, there can be a prayer on your lips. Sing songs of Jesus' love to your little one as you rock him/her to sleep. Repeat your favorite Bible verses while bathing baby. Those things do not take any extra time at all. It is just a different way of interacting with your baby and, at the same time, creates opportunities of prayer, praise, and a chance to remind you of God's promises. So even if you are struggling to find "alone time" with God, take advantage of those small pieces of time all through your day as you go about your parenting responsibilities.

As your child gets older and outgrows those required feedings every few hours, so will your chances to have that alone time. Regular sleep and awake times for your little one will help you have more regular time to devote to your personal spiritual growth in Bible study, personal reflection, and prayer. Time spent in daily Bible study and prayer draws you closer to your heavenly Father. Through prayer you can talk to Him about your parenting joys as well as your parenting challenges. As you read each scripture verse you can read it through the eyes of a parent. Look at each verse you read and reflect on how you may apply that specific verse to parenting. How do the stories speak to you? You will discover words that encourage and words that challenge you to change. Be open to both.

GROUP DISCUSSION

Discuss the statement below. Do you agree with it? Why or why not?

"Raising children pushes parents to mature in their faith as much as it moves children toward spiritual wholeness" (Barna, 2003, p. 85).

WRAP UP

Remember that even if you were not prepared for parenting, or even if it was unplanned, God has entrusted a child to you. He has called you to parent this child. No one can do what God has called you to do. Let Him co-parent with you!

The most important thing you can do to build a strong foundation in your home is to be sure that it is founded upon Jesus. Nourish your relationship with Jesus. Take time daily to spend with Him. Say a prayer as you go about your daily activities. Sing a song of praise to Him.

If married, you also need to spend quality time with your spouse. Even if those moments are few, make them count. Turn off the television and spend time communicating with each other.

If you are reading this, chances are you already have a child. Even if your child was unplanned, it is not too late to build your home on a strong spiritual foundation. Make Jesus the center of your home. Develop a personal relationship with Him. You must be sure that your heart is right with Him before you can transmit those spiritual values to your child. In the next lesson we will look at ways to make Jesus your child's best friend. But before we can build up a child, we need to look at the foundation. Conduct an inspection on the foundation of your "home". Are repairs in order?

BIG THINGS CAN HAPPEN IN SMALL MOMENTS
· Pray while changing your child's diaper.

· Sing songs of Jesus when rocking your baby.

· Repeat Bible verses to them.

· Play a Bible story CD in the car while running errands.

GROUP DISCUSSION

Discuss the statement below. How does it apply to building a firm foundation in our family life? According to the statement, parents have a responsibility to provide instruction to their children in what areas?

"Upon all parents there rests the obligation of giving physical, mental, and spiritual instruction. It should be the object of every parent to secure to his child a well-balanced, symmetrical character. This is a work of no small magnitude and importance—a work requiring earnest thought and prayer no less than patient, persevering effort. A right foundation must be laid, a framework, strong and firm, erected; and then day by day the work of building, polishing, perfecting, must go forward" (Ellen G. White, 1954, p. 17).

GROUP ACTIVITY

Individually list specific ways that you can strengthen the foundation of your home to assure that it is firm. Then, share your responses with the group.

TRY THIS AT HOME
Here are some things to try at home this week:

1. Remember to continue the "Bible Promise Project" we started in chapter one. Find a promise in the Bible that you can apply to building a firm foundation. Write it out on an index card and put it in a prominent place in your home where you can see it throughout the day. Repeat it often, memorize it, and claim it as your own. And, remember to share it the next time you meet with your group members.

2. If you do not currently have personal devotional time, begin this week. If you are married, begin a daily practice of Bible study and prayer with your spouse. A firm foundation may only be built on personal Bible study and prayer.

3. Plan a get-away for some "me time." If you are married, plan a date with your spouse. Take that time to pray, talk together, reconnect with God, and dedicate yourselves as parents to Him.

A PRAYER YOU MAY SAY

Dear Lord, You have called me to parent this child. I understand the importance of making sure the foundation of my home is strong to withstand the storms of life today. The only way that can happen is if my home rests upon You. Today, I dedicate my family to You. Help me to be the kind of parent that You want me to be. Show me ways to strengthen the foundation of my home. In Jesus' name, Amen.

REFERENCES

Adamsons, K. (2013). "Predictors of relationship quality during the transition to parenthood." *Journal of Reproductive and Infant Psychology*, 31(2).

Barna, G. (2003). *Transforming Children into Spiritual Champions*. Ventura, CA: Regal Books.

Bennett, W. (1993). *The Book of Virtues*. New York, NY: Simon & Schuster.

Guttmacher Institute. (September 2013). "Facts on unintended pregnancies in the United States." Retrieved from http://www.guttmacher.org/pubs/FB-Unintended-Pregnancy-US.html Washington, D.C.

Kimmel, T. (2006). *Raising Kids for True Greatness*. Nashville, TN: Thomas Nelson.

Livingston, G. (2013). "At Grandmother's house we stay." Retrieved from http://www.pewsocialtrends.org/2013/09/04/at-grandmothers-house-we-stay/

Morison, A. (2011). "Why your foundation is the most important part of your house." Straw Bale Innovations, LLC. Ashland, OR. Retrieved from http://www.strawbale.com/why-your-foundation-is-the-most-important-part-of-your-house/

Ribar, D. C. (2004, January). *What Do Social Scientists Know About the Benefits of Marriage?: A Review of Quantitative Methodologies*. (IZA Discussion paper series, No. 998. George Washington University and IZA Bonn). Washington, DC: George Washington University. Retrieved from http://ftp.iza.org/dp998.pdf

Thomas, G. (2005). *Devotions for Sacred Parenting*. Grand Rapids, MI: Zondervan.

White, E. G. (1954). *Child Guidance*. Hagerstown, MD: Review and Herald Publishing Association.

White, E. G. (1952). *The Adventist Home*. Hagerstown, MD: Review and Herald Publishing Association.

Wilcox, W. & Drew, J. (2012). "The date night opportunity." *National Marriage Project*. Charlottesville, VA.

HELP! I'M A PARENT FACEBOOK PAGE
Like us on our Facebook page: "Help! I'm a Parent" New materials are posted on a regular basis.

ADDITIONAL MATERIALS FOR CHAPTER 2- FIRM FOUNDATION

These materials are provided as supplemental information to aid in the understanding of development in the young child.

I. KNOWLEDGE OF INDIVIDUAL DEVELOPMENT

What exactly is development? There are as many theories of development as there are schools of developmental thought. Different disciplines approach the study of development from different perspectives.

Development proceeds from the head downward. This is called the "cephalocaudal" principle. This principle describes the direction of growth and development. According to this principle, the child gains control of the head first, then the arms, and then the legs. Infants develop control of the head and face movements within the first two months after birth. In the next few months, they are able to lift themselves up by using their arms. By six to 12 months of age, infants start to gain leg control and may be able to crawl, stand, or walk. Coordination of arms always precedes coordination of legs.

Development proceeds from the center of the body outward. This is the principle of "proximodistal" development that also describes the direction of development. This means that the spinal cord develops before outer parts of the body. The child's arms develop before the hands and the hands and feet develop before the fingers and toes. Finger and toe muscles (used in fine motor dexterity) are the last to develop in physical development.

Development depends on maturation and learning. Maturation refers to the sequential characteristic of biological growth and development. The biological changes occur in sequential order and give children new abilities. There are changes in the brain and nervous system that account largely for maturation. These changes in the brain and nervous system help children to improve in thinking (cognitive) and motor (physical) skills. Also, children must mature to a certain point before they can progress to new skills (Readiness). For example, a four-month-old cannot use language because the infant's brain has not matured enough to allow the child to talk. By two years old, the brain has developed further and with help from others, the child will have the capacity to say and understand words. Also, a child can't write or draw until she has developed the motor control to hold a pencil or crayon. Maturational patterns are innate—that is, genetically programmed. The child's environment and the learning that occurs as a result of the child's experiences largely determine whether the child will reach optimal development. A stimulating environment and varied experiences allow a child to develop to his or her potential.

Development proceeds from the simple (concrete) to the more complex. Children use their cognitive and language skills to reason and solve problems. For example, learning relationships between things (how things are similar) or classification is an important ability in cognitive development. The cognitive process of learning how an apple and orange are alike begins with the most simple or concrete thought of describing the two. Seeing no relationship, a preschool child will describe the objects according to some property of the object, such as color. Such a response would be, "An apple is red (or green) and an orange is orange." The first level of thinking about how objects are alike is to give a description or functional relationship (both concrete thoughts) between the two objects. "An apple and orange are round" and "An apple and orange are alike because you eat them" are typical responses of three, four and five-year-olds. As children develop further in cognitive skills, they are able to understand a higher and more complex relationship between objects and things; that is, that an apple and orange exist in a class called fruit. The child cognitively is then capable of classification.

Growth and development is a continuous process. As a child develops, he or she adds to the skills already acquired and the new skills become the basis for further achievement and mastery of skills. Most children follow a similar pattern. Also, one stage of development lays the foundation for the next stage of development. For example, in motor development, there is a predictable sequence of developments that occur before walking. The infant lifts and turns the head before he or she can turn over. Infants can move their limbs (arms and legs) before grasping an object. Mastery of climbing stairs involves increasing skills from holding onto something to walking alone. By the age of four, most children can walk up and down stairs with alternating feet. As in maturation, in order for children to write or draw, they must have developed the manual (hand) control to hold a pencil and crayon.

Growth and development proceed from the general to specific. In motor development, the infant will be able to grasp an object with the whole hand before using only the thumb and forefinger. The infant's first motor movements are very generalized, undirected, and reflexive, waving arms or kicking before being able to reach or creep toward an object. Growth occurs from large muscle movements to more refined (smaller) muscle movements.

There are individual rates of growth and development. Each child is different and the rates at which individual children grow are different. Although the patterns and sequences for growth and development are usually the same for all children, the rates at which individual children reach developmental stages will be different. Understanding this fact of individual differences in rates of development should cause us to be careful about using and relying on age and stage characteristics to describe or label children. There is a range of ages for any developmental task to take place. This dismisses the notion of the "average child." Some children will walk at ten months while others walk at eighteen months of age. Some children are more active while others are more passive. This does not mean that the passive child will be less intelligent as an adult. There is no validity to comparing one child's progress with or against another child. Rates of development also are not uniform within an individual child. For example, a child's intellectual development may progress faster than his or her emotional or social development.

Development is an ongoing process. Development begins with conception and does not end until death. A broader view of development is that it begins before conception, since the genetic basis for any individual's development is present in the reproductive cells of that individual's parents. This view of development is called "phylogenetic," and it represents the continuous development of life across generations.

Development is a dynamic process.
Development involves continuous
change. Without change, we do not have
development. Sometimes the change is
referred to as "growth."

**Development does not wait for us to be
ready.** Development comes whether one
wants it to or not. In fact, as soon as one
becomes comfortable, there will likely be a
change in development!

Development is directional. Most
developmental processes occur
in predictable, defined directions.
Development typically proceeds from
simple to complex. This is repeated in
all developmental domains. Biologically, any individual begins as a single cell
and develops into a complex organism with millions of cells that are highly
differentiated by both structure and function. These cells are organized into more
and more complex, interacting structures as development proceeds.

The same basic pattern is often repeated, for example, in motor development.
The rudimentary and uncoordinated motor movements of a newborn infant
become increasingly complicated and efficient as the child grows. Complicated
patterns of gross motor skill, fine motor skill, and eye-hand coordination are
precursors to such simple actions as maneuvering through space without injury,
as well as to more complex activities, such as playing basketball.

Development may involve stages. At certain predictable times in the
developmental process, particular tasks or activities emerge. These
developmental points or plateaus are often referred to as stages. Stages may
represent a qualitative change in development. An example is the emergence of
stranger anxiety in an infant who previously was happy being held by anyone.

When the new skill or behavior appears, there is usually a period of leveling off
when the new skills or abilities are practiced, mastered, and integrated into the
child's behavior. For example, after an infant has learned to walk, she may spend
several months perfecting balance, coordination and stability.

Stages may build upon each other. Early tasks and abilities may form the
foundation for later development. For example, the ability to engage in reciprocal
interpersonal relationships is based on trust, a developmental milestone of the
first year of life.

Development is cumulative. Early developmental tasks form the foundation for
the development of later, more complicated tasks. This is a critical concept in
understanding the importance of early recognition and intervention when children
are developmentally delayed.

WHAT IS NORMAL?
Normal is a statistical concept. Normal represents what is typical for the majority
of members of a group. The typical development can be determined in child

HELP! I'M A PARENT WEBSITE
Visit our parenting website to
submit questions, find additional
resources, follow a blog, sign up
for a free parenting e-newsletter,
and more: *www.HelpImAParent.org*

development by observing a representative group of children, by identifying the traits and processes displayed by most children, and by determining the time frames for the emergence of each trait or process.

The rate of a child's development may vary between traits. For example, a child may develop physical skills earlier and language skills later than average but still be within normal limits. Earlier development may, at times, be genetically determined, or it may be promoted in traits or skill areas that are favored and reinforced by the child's culture and environment. Therefore, the term "normal" most appropriately refers to the trait, not the child, and the rate and progress of a child's development must be evaluated individually for each developmental domain.

It is also important to realize that when it comes to family development; normal is still a statistical concept. There are no normal or natural patterns of family development. Since families are made of individuals, their development will be reflective of the development of the people within them (*Adventist Family Ministries Curriculum*, 2012, pp. 30-33).

II. CHILD SEXUAL ANATOMY AND DEVELOPMENT

What do parents or caregivers need to know before they begin to be sex educators at home? A basic understanding of reproductive and sexual anatomy and human development is extremely helpful.

Many adults are uncomfortable with the correct names for sexual anatomy. Some people resort to nicknames for sexual body parts. However, adults need to be comfortable with their own bodies and use language that they can not only communicate clearly with their children but also with medical professionals. Adults are responsible for their own health, as well as their children's, and must be comfortable checking their bodies for breast or prostate cancer, infections, or menstrual abnormalities. If adults use the correct terms such as penis or vagina in a direct and unembarrassed manor, children become more comfortable correctly identifying sexual anatomy and asking questions about their changing bodies.

In addition to knowing about sexual anatomy, it is also very important to know about stages of sexual development for children and teens. Small children may delightedly make "new" discoveries about their bodies and enjoy exploring these discoveries. All children and teens will have questions and concerns about their changing bodies. If parents and caregivers understand what is normal or typical at each stage of a child's development, they can help the child grow into a sexually healthy adult, as well as ease some of the difficulties of growing up and experiencing puberty. Lois Morris, in *Talking Sex With Your Kids*, reminds parents and caregivers that "what kids need—and as it turns out, what they want—is for their parents to explain what all this sex stuff means. They need help making sense of it in terms of their own lives and experiences, and to help them to understand what is ahead for them as boys and girls, men and women" (Morris, 1984, pg. 62, 63).

Preschool Children Less Than 4 Years
· Exploring and touching private parts, in public and in private

· Rubbing private parts (with hand or against objects)

- Showing private parts to others

- Trying to touch mother's or other women's breasts

- Removing clothes and wanting to be naked

- Attempting to see other people when they are naked or undressing (such as in the bathroom)

- Asking questions about their own—and others'—bodies and bodily functions

- Talking to children their own age about bodily functions such as "poop" and "pee"

Young Children Approximately 4-6 Years
- Purposefully touching private parts (masturbation), occasionally in the presence of others

- Attempting to see other people when they are naked or undressing

- Mimicking dating behavior (such as kissing, or holding hands)

- Talking about private parts and using "naughty" words, even when they don't understand the meaning

- Exploring private parts with children their own age (such as "playing doctor", "I'll show you mine if you show me yours," etc). (*Adventist Family Ministries Curriculum*, 2012, pp. 106-107).

REFERENCES

Morris, L. (1984). *Talking Sex With Your Kids*. New York, NY: Simon & Schuster.

North American Division Department of Family Ministries. (2012). *Adventist Family Ministries Curriculum*. Lincoln, NE: Advent*Source*.

3. FOREVER FRIENDSHIP

SCRIPTURAL PRINCIPLE

"No longer do I call you servants, for a servant does not know what his master is doing; but I have called you friends . . . " (John 15:15).

ICEBREAKER—GROUP DISCUSSION

1. REMEMBER

· Who was your best childhood friend? What made them so?

· Are they still your friends? What keeps your friendship intact, healthy, and strong?

2. REVIEW

· Read the entire section of John 15:1-17. How are verses 9 and 12 related to one another?

· How is love the essential dynamic of the Christian life?

· How does our relationship with Jesus change once we understand and start practicing the principle of verse 13?

3. REFLECT

· Do you feel more like Jesus' servant or His friend?

· What might help you to develop a closer friendship with Jesus? What would He have to do? What would you have to do?

OVERVIEW

Our scripture for this chapter reminds us that Jesus Himself calls us His friends. Let's think about what that means. Merriam-Webster (2013) defines a friend as "a person who you like and enjoy being with." Think about that definition in terms of being friends with Jesus. According to the definition, if you are to call Jesus your friend then that means that you must (a) "like" Him and (b) "enjoy being with" Him. The only way that will occur is by spending time with Him.

When we first meet someone, we do not call them friends but acquaintances. It is only as we spend time together that a friendship develops. In John 15, Jesus describes Himself as "The Vine." Friendship is like the attachment that exists between the vine and the branches. It is strengthened and nourished by time.

As we discuss the importance of introducing our children to a forever friendship with Jesus, we will consider the following:

· Modeling
· Family Worship
· Sabbath School, Church Attendance, and Sabbath Afternoons
· Daily Activities
· Benefits to Your Child of a Forever Friendship with Jesus

MODELING

Perhaps you have heard the old adage, "Do as I say—not as I do." Somehow those words fall on deaf ears. Instead, the old adage, "actions speak louder than words" seems to make a lot more sense. This has never been truer than as it relates to the area of parenting. Even very young children mimic what they see. They are the best reflectors of what they observe. So, as we consider the topic of introducing our children to Jesus as their best friend, we must first look in the mirror.

Would your child say that Jesus is your best friend? What would make them answer the way they would? Do you speak of Jesus often in your home? Is He given a place of priority in your family schedule? Is He included in your family celebrations?

GROUP ACTIVITY

Answer each question individually and then share your responses with the group.

1. If you could be personal friends with anyone in the world, who would it be? Why?

2. What is the difference between knowing about someone and knowing them?

3. Do your friendships reflect your values? If so, in what ways?

If you want Jesus to be your child's best friend, then He must first be *your* best friend. This must be evidenced in all that you do. Jesus must be central to all you do as a family. Your child must know that Jesus is a treasured family member in the same way as grandma or grandpa. They will hold Jesus in the same place of priority in the family as you give to Him.

"The stakes you face as a parent are much too great to go unnoticed by a God who loves you—and your children" (Thomas, 2005, p. 14).

FAMILY WORSHIP

Your family priorities are reflected in the way you spend your family time. What place does Jesus have in your home? Is the sum total contained in the few hours that you spend as a family in church each week? Or, is He a part of everyday activities?

As a family, you may readily recognize the value of proper nutrition, water, sunlight, rest, and other daily activities. Your bodies need those things in order to be healthy. In the same way, you also need spiritual nourishment. Your family is nourished spiritually only through time spent with Jesus. He must be central to all that is done in your home.

Family worship should be a part of every day. It should be every day and at the same time every day. Be consistent and do not allow the busyness of your daily life to push it aside. Remember, it should not be hours in length. The point is to make sure that worship activities are age appropriate for your child. A half hour of reading from the book of Revelation in the Bible may not be especially appealing to a two-year-old. Instead, try reading a short story from their favorite Bible storybook, playing a Bible game, putting a Bible puzzle together, and talking about the story as you help your child put the puzzle pieces in place. Spend time in nature by collecting colorful fall leaves or bird watching and talk to your child about God as the Creator. These types of age appropriate activities make family worship something your child will look forward to all day long. Make it varied to keep it interesting. Have it indoors one day and outdoors the next, if weather permits. When they are older, involve them in the planning. You may be amazed at what they will come up with.

"Train up a child in the way he should go, And when he is old he will not depart from it" Proverbs 22:6.

As a parent, do you want your child to grow up to be an active member in your church? If so, consider this research. Benson and Eklin (1990) discovered that children who are most likely to mature in faith are those raised in homes where faith is part of the normal ebb and flow of family life. Religious practices in the home virtually double the probability of a child growing up to be an active member of the church. In other words, what happens in your home affects their involvement in the church when they grow to be adults. The "normal ebb and flow of family life" today will affect them tomorrow. They must see Jesus in your everyday life at home in order to care about church attendance as they grow to make decisions on their own. This means that time spent in daily family worship as a child will set the stage for adult behavior later on.

SABBATH SCHOOL, CHURCH ATTENDANCE, AND SABBATH AFTERNOONS

Scripture calls the Sabbath "a delight" (Isaiah 58:13). Would your child call it the

FAMILY WORSHIP FUN

· Read a short story from their favorite Bible story book.

· Play a Bible game.

· Put a Bible puzzle together – talk about the story as you put the puzzle together with your child.

· Write and illustrate Bible verses and frame them to hang on the walls.

same? It is far too easy to fill the Sabbath with a list of "don'ts" and things that "are not allowed." Instead, make it a delight that it was intended to be, not just for your children, but also for your entire family. All week talk about how you look forward to the Sabbath. Talk about the special meal, the family outing in nature, or the opportunity to see a beloved friend again. Your attitude about the Sabbath will be contagious. If the day is a delight for you, it will also become a delight for your child. On the other hand, if you speak negatively about the day, so will your child.

It may be very tempting to stay at home on Sabbath instead of going to church. Maybe it has been a tough week at work and you would relish the idea of sleeping in a few extra hours or lounging around the house all day. And, have you noticed how Satan does everything possible on Sabbath mornings to create havoc in your home? The bathtub overflows, the toast burns, the dress shoes need polishing, and your little girl's Sabbath dress is ripped. Oh, it is so tempting to stay at home! The extra effort of getting little ones up, fed, and dressed in nice clothes is exhausting before you even walk out of the door.

But creating a habit of church attendance is important in raising Godly children. A habit formed in childhood is often continued into adulthood. As a result, if a child attends church regularly, they will likely continue to attend when they grow older. You cannot expect teenagers to want to go to church if they never developed a love for it as toddlers. Remember, your parenting efforts are not only for today's challenges. Rather, you are training for tomorrow's decisions also.

Perhaps one of a child's favorite things about Sabbath is going to Sabbath School. It is there that they can sing the songs that appeal to them, listen to Bible stories told in age-appropriate ways, ring the bells, and play with the colorful felt pieces. It also gives children the opportunity to socialize with a peer group that shares their family faith values. Now, this also means leaving the home even earlier than if you were only going to attend the worship service and listen to the sermon. But put yourself in your child's shoes when you are tempted to do this. In so doing, your child would be missing out on perhaps one of the best parts of the day. If you were a toddler, wouldn't you want to be in Sabbath School? That's where the fun is!

"Call the Sabbath a delight, the holy day of the LORD honorable" Isaiah 58:13.

Don't forget that the Sabbath day does not end with the benediction after the church service. You still have half the day left. And even though your little one may need to nap in the afternoon, that still leaves several hours in the day to fill with appropriate Sabbath activities. That is a great time of the week to plan a special outing as an entire family. Fill every second of it with quality time to reconnect to God and to each other as family members. Ask your child for ideas.

Allow them input in to how to spend the time. Keep a stack of special toys or games reserved only for the Sabbath hours. In this way those toys are special and not something that they get to play with every other day of the week. Purchase a special container and fill it with Bible puzzles, games, coloring books, Bible storybooks, etc.

One way to make the Sabbath a delight is to plan special meals. In our home, this was the one day of the week when we had a special dessert. We called it our "Sabbath Treat." We also had special candles on the table, reserved for Sabbath, that our little girls got to light on Friday evening as the sun was going down. And that special container came out that was labeled, "Sabbath Toys." Those simple things made the Sabbath a delight for our little girls. Instead of it being a day filled with a list of things they could not do, it was a day filled with special privileges reserved just for the Sabbath.

GROUP ACTIVITY

1. Read the following texts: Genesis 2:1, Exodus 20:8-11, and Mark 2:27. What do you believe are the benefits God intended for us as we rest on the Sabbath?

2. List specific ways that the Sabbath can be made a delight for each member of your family.

DAILY ACTIVITIES

Making Jesus our child's best friend is not something that happens if we only go to church on Sabbath. In realty, this happens by being intentional every day of the week. It happens through the small things that we incorporate into our daily activities.

Prayer is one of those things. Yes, it means praying at mealtimes, even if we are in a family restaurant, but prayer also should happen at other times during the day. You can intentionally teach your child to take all matters to Jesus in prayer. For example, if your child is having trouble finding a favorite stuffed animal or blanket, you can kneel with them and pray to Jesus to help them find it. Then, when it is found, you can take a moment to kneel with them again and offer a prayer of thanksgiving. You can pause at numerous times during their day to help them pray about their joys as well as their frustrations. Soon it will become a habit for them to talk to Jesus on their own. It takes those few extra minutes, but when it is a habit instilled in them, you will know that every minute you spent was priceless and nothing else was of more importance.

> "Brief prayers keep you plugged into God's wisdom" (Kuzma, 2006, p. 37).

Keep an open eye for those "teachable moments" that will occur unexpectedly all during your normal daily routine. When you are stuck in a traffic jam and your child is in the backseat crying in their car seat, start singing a song to Jesus that they are familiar with. When you see the first flower bloom in the springtime, take a moment and talk to your child about what it must have been like for Jesus on that third day of creation when He made all the beautiful, colorful flowers. Those moments fill our day, and all you need to do is to ask God to point them out to you and to help you in not allowing them to pass.

GROUP ACTIVITY

Answer these individually, then share your responses with the group.

1. If you lived in Jesus' time, what would you tell your children about Him?

2. What are your favorite stories about Jesus that would make Him real to your child?

BENEFITS TO YOUR CHILD OF HAVING A FOREVER FRIENDSHIP WITH JESUS

What are the benefits of making Jesus your child's forever friend? Studies show the beneficial results of religious belief and practice on physical and mental health and on relationships. It appears that one of the most important things parents can do for their children is to have a Christ-centered home (Dollahite and Thatcher, 2005, p. 10). A growing body of empirical research demonstrates that a family's religious involvement directly benefits children in a variety of significant ways.

In their survey of the research literature, David Dollahite and Jennifer Thatcher (2005) found the following benefits of a family's religious involvement:

- Divorce rates are lower and marital satisfaction and quality scores highest among religiously involved couples.

- Religious practices are linked with family satisfaction, closer father-child relationships, and closer parent-child relationships.

- There is less domestic violence among more religious couples, and religious parents are less likely to abuse or yell at their children.

- Religious involvement promotes involved and responsible fathering and is associated with more involved mothering.

- Greater religiosity in parents and youth is inversely related with many high-risk behaviors, all of which have potential to greatly influence current and future family relationships.

Yes, Jesus wants a forever friendship with you and with your child. The benefits to your child are numerous. Here are some ways a forever friendship with Jesus will benefit your child:

1. **It promotes their eternal happiness.** When your child has Jesus as their friend, they will discover joy in Jesus Christ. They will understand that true lasting happiness is not in all the "stuff" the world has to offer, but in knowing Jesus.

2. **It helps them make sense out of life.** Your child will come to understand God as the Creator, how sin entered the world, God's gift of salvation, and look forward to their heavenly home.

A BOOK FOR PARENTS TO INTRODUCE YOUR CHILD TO JESUS:

Making Jesus My Best Friend

- Written by Drs. Claudio & Pamela Consuegra

- Available in English & Spanish

- from Advent*Source*, Review & Herald, or on ***Amazon.com***

3. **It's their best chance to accept Christ.**
Research has proven that children tend to be more receptive to the gospel than any other age group. Take advantage of those young years to introduce your little ones to Jesus.

4. **It can help counter balance worldly influences.** Children need positive influences to tip the scale in this secularized world. A friendship with Jesus helps them focus on the spiritual rather than the secular.

5. **It can help them learn to love others.**
The second greatest commandment is to love your neighbor. We must teach this as a way of life, because it doesn't come naturally. A love for Jesus flows out to others.

> "The cause of division and discord in families and in the church is separation from Christ. To come near to Christ is to come near to one another. The secret of true unity in the church and in the family is not diplomacy, not management, not a superhuman effort to overcome difficulties—though there will be much of this to do—but union with Christ" (White, 1952, p. 179).

6. **It is something fun to do.** Do you know who invented fun? God did. Do you know why? For His own glory. While entertainment and fun seeking can become an idol, we should not think God is against fun. Being friends with Jesus is fun, and it is your responsibility as a parent to focus on the joy of service, the beauty in nature, and the happiness that comes from knowing Jesus.

7. **It helps them with their relationships/friendships.** Exposing your child to those who share your family faith values will assist them in their choice of friends. This is a key benefit to your child as you have the opportunity to guide them in establishing positive relationships.

8. **It gives children special memories.** Think back to when you were a child. Can you remember a special Sabbath School teacher or other church-related event? Things like crafts made in Vacation Bible School and songs learned in Sabbath School can become a lasting memory. Or perhaps it is a favorite family worship activity or the way that you said family prayers. When Jesus is your child's best friend, you expose them to many memory-making opportunities.

> "If we lose sight of that judgment day, we risk missing the ultimate purpose of parenting and thus find we've wasted our energy focusing on lesser aims. It's not that we don't care about manners, athletics, grades, and social acceptance; but we remember that our greatest call is to lead our children to righteousness. When they stand alone before God, it won't matter how early in life they were potty trained; we won't care whether they could run a mile in four minutes or shoot below par in a round of golf; it won't matter if they earned a six-figure income or died with a six-figure debt or could fit into a size 2 dress. What will matter is that they take their place alongside us in the glorious reality God calls heaven" (Thomas, 2005, p. 109).

9. It allows them to make friends with adult volunteers in a safe environment. In our culture, child safety is a constant concern—and rightly so. But there is still great value in kids finding trusted adults. Your practices as a family will expose them to significant adults such as a pastor, Sabbath School teacher, or other family friend.

GROUP DISCUSSION

1. What is the length of your longest friendship? What has kept you as friends for that long?

2. Has somebody else ever tried to come between you and your friend? What did you do to prevent that from happening?

3. What can you apply from your earthly friendships to your friendship with Jesus? What can you teach your children?

4. Think about some of the friendships mentioned in the Bible (Ruth/Naomi; David/Jonathan; Paul/Barnabas; David/Hananiah, Mishael, and Azariah). What can you learn from them? What do they have in common?

WRAP UP

A forever friendship with Jesus for your child actually begins with you. Take some time for self-reflection. Would your child say that Jesus is *your* best friend?

Daily family worship may seem like another thing to add to an already over-scheduled day. Consider ways you can enhance the experience for your family and make it something the children eagerly anticipate all during the day.

Attendance at Sabbath School and church on a regular basis is important to the spiritual health of the entire family. Sabbath afternoons are a special time to enjoy each others' company and to connect with Jesus.

Common daily activities provide numerous opportunities to teach your child about Jesus. As a parent you need to be open and look for those moments and not allow them to pass. Ultimately, by having a forever relationship with Jesus Christ, your child will experience benefits that will last a lifetime and carry them through eternity.

GROUP DISCUSSION

Discuss the statement below. How does it speak to you, as a parent, about leading your child to a forever friendship with Jesus Christ?

"The work of education in the home, if it is to accomplish all that God designs it shall, demands that parents be diligent students of the Scriptures. They must be learners of the great Teacher. Day by day the law of love and kindness must be upon their lips. Their lives must reveal the grace and truth that was seen in the life of their Example. Then a sanctified love will bind the hearts of parents and children together, and the youth will grow up established in the faith and rooted and grounded in the love of God" (White, 1954, p. 66).

GROUP ACTIVITY

Answer these individually and then share your responses with the group.

List some specific ways that you can help your child develop a "Forever Friendship" with Jesus.

TRY THIS AT HOME
Here are some things to try at home this week:

1. Remember to continue the "Bible Promise Project" we started in chapter one. Find a promise in the Bible that you can apply to helping your child have a forever friendship with Jesus. Write it out on an index card and put it in a prominent place in your home where you can see it throughout the day. Repeat it often, memorize it, and claim it as your own. And remember to share it the next time you meet with your group members.

2. Begin putting together some toys, games, etc. that will be reserved just for the Sabbath. Label it "My Sabbath Bag" and fill it with various age-appropriate items. Remember, if you allow your child to play with it during the week, you will defeat the purpose.

3. If you are not having family worship, start today. Keep it at a consistent time every day, keep it short, and remember to make the worship activity age appropriate, enjoyable, and exciting for your child.

4. Look for those "teachable moments" this week and use them as opportunities to talk about Jesus.

A PRAYER YOU MAY SAY
Dear Lord, I want my child to have a forever friendship with You. I know that it starts with me. Help me to reflect You to my child. Help me to be faithful in being a positive Christian role model. Help me to be a spiritual leader in my home, initiating daily family worship and prayer. Help me to be faithful in church attendance. May words of praise and love to You be spoken so often in my home that it is obvious You are a precious part of our family circle. And help my child to see You as their very best friend. In Jesus' name, Amen.

REFERENCES

Bennett, W. (1993). *The Book of Virtues*. New York, NY: Simon & Schuster.

Benson, P. and Eklin, C. (1990). *Effective Christian Education: A Summary Report on Faith, Loyalty, and Congregational Life*. Minneapolis, MN: Search Institute.

Dollahite, D. and Thatcher, J. (2005). *How Family Religious Involvement Benefits Adults, Youth, and Children and Strengthens Families*. The Sutherland Institute. Retrieved from: www.sutherlandinstitute.org/blog/how-family-strengthens-families/

Kuzma, K, (2008) *The First 7 Years*. Pacific Press Publishing. Nampa, Idaho.

Merriam-Webster Web. (n.d.). *Merriam-Webster.com*. Retrieved (6 Oct. 2013) from http://www.merriam-webster.com/dictionary/friend

Thomas, G. (2005). *Devotions for Sacred Parenting*. Grand Rapids, MI: Zondervan.

White, E. G. (1954). *Child Guidance*. Hagerstown, MD: Review and Herald Publishing Association.

White, E. G. (1952). *The Adventist Home*. Hagerstown, MD: Review and Herald Publishing Association.

HELP! I'M A PARENT WEBSITE

Visit our parenting website to submit questions, find additional resources, follow a blog, sign up for a free parenting e-newsletter, and more: ***www.HelpImAParent.org***

HELP! I'M A PARENT FACEBOOK PAGE

Like us on our Facebook page: "Help! I'm a Parent" New materials are posted on a regular basis.

Help! I'm a Parent: Christian Parenting in the Real World

4. SHARING AND SERVICE

SCRIPTURAL PRINCIPLE

"Yet it shall not be so among you; but whoever desires to become great among you, let him be your servant. And whoever desires to be first among you, let him be your slave—just as the Son of Man did not come to be served, but to serve, and to give His life a ransom for many" (Matthew 20:26-28).

ICEBREAKER—GROUP DISCUSSION

1. REMEMBER
- What did your parents want you to be when you grew up? What did you want to be when you grew up?

- What are some secret hopes and expectations you have for your children?

2. REVIEW
- How do you feel about competition?

- What do the verses of the scriptural principle teach about the way things are done in the world and how God desires us to do things instead?

3. REFLECT
- How significant do you feel as a part of God's kingdom?

- What are some specific ways you can be of service to those in your family, following Jesus' pattern? To other people?

OVERVIEW

Self-centeredness seems to be inherent. Isaiah portrays Lucifer's desire to be number one (Isaiah 14:13-14). Human nature seems to have inherited that trait from the father of lies. How do you teach your child to put God first in a me-first society? As much as you try, it seems that society is a counterproductive force. Sports figures teach that you must win in order to have significance. Video games drill competition with every move. Schools require top scores in order to be accepted and at work you have to fight to keep your job. The questions you are being taught to ask is not how you can spend your life in ways to benefit others, but what can you get out of life for yourself.

As a Christian parent, you want to train your child to have an unselfish, generous spirit—to be giving and willing to be involved in Christian service to others! You want your children to joyfully and willingly give of themselves and serve others for the rest of their lives. How can you teach your children to put others before themselves? How can you help them experience the joy that comes when we bless others?

> "God uses parenting to shape and mold us into his servants. We must learn not only how to love compliant people but also how to love difficult people, overly active people, strong-willed people, and even, on occasion, cruel people" (Thomas, 2005, p. 57).

As we consider teaching children the importance of sharing and service, we will consider the following:

- Sharing with siblings/peers
- Service projects
- Teaching an attitude of gratitude

> "Gratitude is important not only because it helps us feel good but also because it inspires us to do good" (Emmons, 2013, p. vii).

SHARING WITH SIBLINGS/PEERS

The first place your child will learn to share with others is in the home. The reality is that sharing is a choice the child will need to make. They may choose to share a toy with their brother or sister, part of their candy bar, or a turn in a game. Sharing does not always come naturally. It is natural for a small child to tightly hold onto that beloved doll, stuffed animal, or toy truck to protect the few belongings they have.

If you have an only child, they may be presented with the choice to share at the babysitter's house, in daycare, or when their cousins or friends come for a visit. Guiding a toddler to the point where they can share easily may take a while. Learning to share, like other refined social skills, takes time and requires constant attention. The key is to start early. As soon as your child can say "mine," they will be able to learn the difference between what's really "mine" and what belongs to someone else.

Laura Stanley (1999) has some practical tips to help young children learn to share:

1. **Make sure your child has lots of play dates.** Children who have no siblings or limited contact with other children tend to have more trouble learning to share. When it comes to sharing, practice makes perfect. Play dates are an opportunity for your child to put their sharing skills to the test.

2. **Help your child learn to negotiate.** Young children do better with hands-on examples. It's much clearer to say, "You've had that ball a long time. Kevin's been waiting. It's time for his turn now." Then, follow through. When Kevin is finished with the ball, point out, "Look, he's finished. You can have it back now." The lesson learned is twofold: "Kevin has feelings like yours, and what belongs to you will ultimately be returned." In this way we help our child learn to negotiate by showing them how it's done. You can even set a timer. In this way they learn the give and take of sharing.

3. **Help your child choose what they are willing to share.** A toddler's anguish can be particularly acute if playmates touch their most precious things, like the bear she sleeps with or something that's special because it's new. Keep these treasures out of sight or tuck them away before others come over to play.

TOO MUCH STUFF?
Does your child have a lot of toys they no longer play with? Perhaps you may help them select one good toy or game to give away to a needy child for their birthday, for Christmas, or for no specific occasion at all.

4. **Control the "grabbies."** Put your young child's feelings into words for him. For example, say, "I understand that you want that toy right now. But Jessica wants it too. You can have a turn when she's finished." Help them learn to use words instead of grabbing to convey their feelings to other children.

4

5. **Sharing, of course, begins with you.** Share with your spouse or other household members in front of your child. Use sharing words often in the home. Point out when others share, and teach your toddler to thank children who share their things with them. And don't forget to praise your own child when they are sharing. Appropriate praise will reinforce the behavior you are trying to teach. Soon sharing will just be a part of normal play.

SERVICE PROJECTS

Do you want your child to have a "servant's heart?" Guess what—It starts with you. "Studies reveal that youth who say their parents 'spent lots of time helping others' are almost twice as likely themselves to serve others. Among young people whose parents model helping, 61 percent volunteer at least one hour per week. Among those whose parents do not model helping, only 36 percent volunteer. People who live lives of service, often point to early childhood experiences in their family as being normative" (Dollahite and Thatcher, 2005, p. 2). In other words, if you want your child to grow up to become a caring, compassionate, and giving adult, then you must start now by modeling that same behavior.

Have your kids seen God's hands? The Bible is a great place to start teaching them the joy of serving others. You can talk about the cross, Jesus washing the disciple's feet, and when Jesus fed crowds of people. Even before children are old enough to actually participate in service activities, you can tell them the beautiful stories in the Bible about serving. But those are just bedtime stories to children who don't witness servant behavior in their world. As they grow they will need to participate, and then those Bible stories will become real in their life as they apply the principles and experience the joy that serving brings.

If your child learns to serve, then kindness is the most natural trait to surface. Kindness will then be followed with respect and responsibility. Serving opens the platform for compassion and love. Serving gets your eyes off of yourself and onto someone else. Serving sets the stage for growth, maturity and blessings. Not that we want to teach our children to serve

SERVICE PROJECTS YOU MAY DO WITH YOUR CHILD:

· Visit a nursing home on a regular basis and arrange to adopt an older person as your child's surrogate grandparent. Together you can make cards, sing songs to them, prepare a special treat, or take them outside for some sunshine and fresh air (please make sure to check with the nursing home ahead of time).

· Volunteer with a hospice program and arrange to take your children along to visit the patients. Many terminally ill patients are practically isolated from friends who are afraid to visit them, not knowing what to do or what to say. Seeing you, and your children, may be a welcome sight for them. At the same time, your children will learn lessons of service and also learn about dying as a normal part of life.

· Buy them a small, plastic, toy rake and broom and take them with you to rake the yard of an elderly person, or to help clean up around the church or a city park.

in exchange for what they will get out of it, but the benefits and blessings we reap are a natural result of serving others.

This series focuses on the young child. That's where the challenge of serving comes in. They are too young to be involved in overseas mission trips or even in a local community service project. They are too small to move furniture, paint park benches, or help construct an orphanage in a far away land. So what's a parent to do? The challenge is in finding age-appropriate activities in which they can participate.

WORKING BY MY FATHER'S SIDE

As I feverishly pushed the lawn mower around our yard, I wondered if I'd finish before dinner. Mikey, our 6-year-old, walked up and, without even asking, stepped in front of me and placed his hands on the mower handle. Knowing that he wanted to help me, I quit pushing.

The mower quickly slowed to a stop. Chuckling inwardly at his struggles, I resisted the urge to say, "Get out of here, kid. You're in my way," and said instead, "Here, Son. I'll help you." As I resume pushing, I bowed my back and leaned forward, and walked spread-legged to avoid colliding with Mikey. The grass cutting continued, but more slowly, and less efficiently than before, because Mikey was "helping" me.

Suddenly, tears came to my eyes as it hit me: This is the way my heavenly Father allows me to "help" him build his kingdom! I pictured my heavenly Father at work seeking, saving, and transforming the lost, and there I was, with my weak hands "helping." My Father could do the work by himself, but he doesn't. He chooses to stoop gracefully to allow me to co-labor with him. Why? For my sake, because he wants me to have the privilege of ministering with Him. (Larson, 1993).

In actuality, service opportunities are all around you. Perhaps we need to take a new look at what serving means to a young child. Here are some things to keep in mind:

1. **Keep it simple.** Service to a young child may be as simple as them helping you pick up toys in the children's room at church. Even picking up a piece of trash on the sidewalk can be a way to serve the community. Start small and keep it simple. This does not have to take hours of time. Just look for simple things that are all around you every day. Talk with them about how the small acts of service are benefiting someone else.

2. **Reflect on the experience.** Talk with your child about what they did. Help them put into words how it felt to help someone else. It is important to take a few minutes to do this. How did it make you feel, your child feel, or how did it make the recipient of the act feel? They will then connect service to benefiting everyone involved.

3. **Give thanks for the opportunity to serve.** Remember to help your child pray and give thanks to Jesus for giving them the opportunity to serve others. Also, help them pray for Jesus to show them new ways that they can serve.

Once your child has experienced the joy of serving, they will likely look for other opportunities themselves. It is your responsibility to support them in volunteerism and to engage in service with them. Families who serve together reap the rewards together.

GROUP DISCUSSION

Do you agree with the following statement? Why or why not?

"According to Jesus, if we want our kids to be truly great, we must first teach them to be servants" (Kimmel, 2006, p. 2).

TEACHING AN ATTITUDE OF GRATITUDE

Teaching our children the joy of sharing and service begins with helping them to be grateful for all God has given them. An unwillingness to share begins with a selfish spirit, while serving others begins with a realization that because you are so blessed, you need to give back and share with others. So teaching our children to have an "attitude of gratitude" from their earliest years will help them put the needs of others first.

Gratitude is the link to giving. Robert Emmons (2013) says, "Gratitude is important not only because it helps us feel good but also because it inspires us to do good" (p. vii). In other words, being grateful propels us to give. It motivates us to action.

So, if being grateful will assist your child in sharing and service, how is it taught? What are some practical ways that you can teach this to the young child? Here are some simple ways to cultivate an attitude of gratitude in young children:

> "Children should be taught to do some little errand of love and mercy for those less fortunate than themselves" (White, 1952, p. 485).

1. **Help your children make a "Thankful Book."** Even young children can do this. They can draw pictures on the pages of things that they are thankful for while you label them. They could also cut pictures out of magazines and glue them in the book. This can be a fun thing to do as a family worship activity or on a Sabbath afternoon. Week by week and year by year the book will grow and you will need to add new volumes to your "Thankful Book." As your child grows, so will their spirit of gratitude. Looking back through this book years later will bring back many family memories. It will be a treasured keepsake.

2. **Appreciate the big things and the little things.** Gratitude can mean being grateful for being born, or being grateful for specific things such as a new puppy, doll, or toy. All of this counts in practicing gratitude with your kids. Help your child by not only pointing out the big things in life for which to be thankful but by noticing the small things also.

3. **Stop and smell the roses.** Take the time to point out blessings to your child. Don't hurry through the day without stopping to smell a flower and thank Jesus for His gifts that are all around us. Soon, your child will be taking note of things to be thankful for on their own. Those few moments are time well spent.

4. **Have your child tell you three good things when you put them to bed each night.** This should relate to things that happened to them that day or that they did during the day. This gives them the lens of gratitude glasses. Practicing this routine at the end of the day will help teach your children to slow down, savor the moment, and notice things they appreciate and should be thankful for. If you make this a nighttime routine, they will

4 WAYS TO PRAISE YOUR CHILD:

1. **Praise Them Selectively**- If you praise them for everything they do, good or bad, it only confuses them. Be selective and praise them for specific, positive behavior.

2. **Praise Them Immediately**- Young children have a short attention span so it is important that you catch your children in the act of doing a good deed and praise them at that time. If you delay your praise until a later time it will have less meaning and power than immediate praise.

3. **Praise Them Specifically**- To say things like "thank you for being a good boy," or I'm glad you were being a nice girl" do not have the same impact as saying things like, "I love the way you shared your toy with your sister," or "What a good job you did making your bed today!" Be specific with your praise.

4. **Praise Them Intentionally**- Look for ways to praise a child with a goal in mind. When you want your children to learn to be kind, praise acts of kindness. Expect your children to be kind and tell them you are not at all surprised at their kind behavior.

(Richard and Rita Tate, 2002)

be expecting it and will be looking for things throughout their day to share with you in the evening. It also helps them go to bed with a positive attitude as they count their blessings.

5. **Write thank-you letters.** Help your child write a letter to somebody like a teacher, neighbor, or another family member who has done something special for him or her. They can dictate for you if they're younger, and then draw a picture. Then take them to deliver it in person, and read it out loud. This teaches them to say thank you and to appreciate others' actions, and not taking them for granted.

WRAP UP

When it comes to teaching our children the importance of sharing, the joy that serving others can bring, and to have an attitude of gratitude, it all has to start at home. First, we must model the behavior. That means we have to get up off the couch and participate in service activities with our child. In addition, words of gratitude must be constantly spoken in our homes and witnessed by our children. A thankful spirit is contagious to them.

GROUP DISCUSSION

Discuss the statement below. How does it apply to you as you teach your child the importance of sharing and serving? What does it mean to "awaken the spirit" of service? How do you "encourage and direct it"?

"Above any other agency, service for Christ's sake in the little things of everyday experience has power to mold the character and to direct the life into lines of unselfish ministry. To awaken this spirit, to encourage and rightly to direct it, is the parents' and the teacher's work. No more important work could be committed to them. The spirit of ministry is the spirit of heaven, and with every effort to develop and encourage it angels will co-operate" (White, 1954, p. 296).

GROUP ACTIVITY

List some service projects that are age-appropriate for young children.

TRY THIS AT HOME
Here are some things to try at home this week:

1. Remember to continue the "Bible Promise Project" we started in chapter one. Find a promise in the Bible that you can apply to teaching your child the importance of sharing and service. Write it out on an index card and put it in a prominent place in your home where you can see it throughout the day. Repeat it often, memorize it, and claim it as your own. And remember to share it the next time you meet with your group members.

2. Chose one service project and set a date to do it together as a family. You may need to search for some community-based needs, but don't give up.

3. Look agin at the suggestions to teach an attitude of gratitude. Select one or two and try it at home this week. Or you may try another on your own.

A PRAYER YOU MAY SAY
Lord, you taught us the importance of serving others. You came to us with a servant's heart. Please help me teach this to my child. Provide opportunities where I can lead my child to show others Your love and in so doing, he/she will experience the joy that giving brings. In Jesus' name, Amen.

REFERENCES

Dollahite, D. and Thatcher, J. (2005). *How Family Religious Involvement Benefits Adults, Youth, and Children and Strengthens Families.* Salt Lake City, UT: The Sutherland Institute. Retrieved from: www.sutherlandinstitute.org

Emmons, R. (2013). *Gratitude Works.* San Francisco, CA: Jossey-Bass Publishers.

Kimmel, T. (2006). *Raising Kids for True Greatness.* Nashville, TN: Thomas Nelson.

Larson, C. B., (1994). *Illustrations for Preaching & Teaching From Leadership Journal.* Grand Rapids, MI: Baker Books.

Stanley, L. (1999, October). "Teaching the joys of sharing." *Parents Magazine.*

Tate, R. and R. (2002). *11 Reasons Families Succeed.* Tulsa, OK: Hensley Publishing.

Thomas, G. (2005). *Devotions for Sacred Parenting.* Grand Rapids, MI: Zondervan.

White, E. G. (1954). *Child Guidance.* Hagerstown, MD: Review and Herald Publishing Association.

White, E. G. (1952). *The Adventist Home.* Hagerstown, MD: Review and Herald Publishing Association.

HELP! I'M A PARENT WEBSITE
Visit our parenting website to submit questions, find additional resources, follow a blog, sign up for a free parenting e-newsletter, and more: ***www.HelpImAParent.org***

HELP! I'M A PARENT FACEBOOK PAGE
Like us on our Facebook page: "Help! I'm a Parent" New materials are posted on a regular basis.

5. RELATIONS AND RIVALRY

SCRIPTURAL PRINCIPLE
"Where do wars and fights come from among you? Do they not come from your desires for pleasure that war in your members?" (James 4:1).

ICEBREAKER—GROUP DISCUSSION

1. REMEMBER
· Who did you quarrel with the most when you were a kid? What did you quarrel over?

2. REVIEW
· Looking at the section of James 4:1-3, from what does this strife come?

· James lists antidotes in James 4:7-10. How does it address the issue of conflict stated earlier?

3. REFLECT
· What is your usual response when your desires are frustrated?

OVERVIEW
One of the most important things you will teach your child is how to build and maintain positive relationships. This is a skill they will carry with them throughout their lifetime, and it is important that it be mastered. It will impact their interactions with peers, academic success, future marital satisfaction, and career success, to mention a few. Relational skills are learned from birth. How do you teach all of the important aspects that surround relational issues?

As we discuss teaching our children positive relational skills, we will consider:

· Modeling Positive Relational Skills
· Sibling Rivalry
· Relationships with Peers
· Bullying

MODELING POSITIVE RELATIONAL SKILLS
Like all of the other parenting principles, teaching your children positive relational skills begins with you. Your relationships with others, positive and negative, will set the stage for them. If married, the way you communicate with your spouse will be mirrored in the relationships they have. The way you handle conflicts will be the same way they approach challenges. If unmarried, you will model relational skills by the way you relate to your own parents, siblings, and others.

"If we would have our children practice kindness, courtesy, and love, we ourselves must set them the example" (White, 1952, p. 421).

In other words, all your relationships are lessons that you teach your child. Your child is watching, listening, and learning every day. Think about these things:

· How do you talk to your spouse?

- How do you relate to your own family members (parents, brothers, sisters)?
- How do you speak about those you work with?
- How do you speak regarding the church?
- How do you solve family conflict?

> Positive attention is better than negative attention, but negative attention is better than no attention at all.

SIBLING RIVALRY

As upsetting and frustrating as this can be for parents, it is unfortunately very common. If you have more than one child, chances are you will have to deal with sibling rivalry. Sibling rivalry is as old as Cain and Abel in the Bible. If allowed, your home can seem like a battlefield, and all your time can be consumed with breaking up fights.

So what's a parent to do? Grace Stopani (2003) gives practical advice to combat sibling rivalry.

1. **Teach mutual respect.** Do not allow your children to insult one another. Words are extremely powerful, and snide comments can cause deep damage. Experts say every negative comment needs at least five positive remarks to even out. Teach your children to be kind and to appreciate each other.

2. **Do not play favorites.** The Bible has some stark examples of parents who played favorites. In Genesis, we see the damage done by Sarah, Abraham's wife, showing preference to Isaac, her biological son, over Ishmael, Abraham's biological son (Genesis 21). While Esau and Jacob were twins, Rebecca, their mother, favored Jacob, while Isaac, their father, favored Esau (Genesis 27). In the next generation, Jacob, who had twelve sons and one daughter, clearly showed preference for Joseph (Genesis 37). Remember that all children are created equal, but not all children are the same. Recognize and praise each child's individual skills, strengths, and accomplishments without implying that one child is somehow better.

3. **Teach conflict management.** Do not deny your child's feelings, but help him or her learn to express emotions in an appropriate way. If you see your child acting out of jealously, encourage him or her to identify the emotion by saying, "I understand that you feel bad because . . ." or "I know you are hurt because . . ." Helping your children figure out the causes of their actions will help them learn how to deal with problems in the future.

4. **Do not ignore good behavior.** To attention-starved kids, negative attention is simply attention. Notice your children playing nicely together and reward them with praise. Be sure each child receives adequate parental interest and quality time.

5. **Show appreciation for who your child is, not what he or she does.** When children feel valuable merely for their performance, they will feel the need to prove their worth. Instead, praise your child for his or her God-given traits, such as compassion or a tender heart. By fostering their self-esteem, children can learn to respect themselves and others.

The reality is that combating sibling rivalry in your home will take a great deal of prayer combined with patience. It will not dissolve overnight. Be consistent and persistent. Using the above strategies will go a long way in teaching your child to manage conflict with brother or sister.

RELATIONSHIPS WITH PEERS

"Play nicely." "Please share with Johnny/Suzie." These or similar phrases are familiar to many of us. You heard them when you were a child and now repeat them to your own child. It's in the early years when you begin to help your child make friends and build relationships. Practicing positive relational skills will help them later as they go to elementary school, high school, college, and begin their careers. In essence, the presence or lack of positive relational skills will have lifelong implications.

Even if you have an only child, they will need to learn how to have positive interactions with their peer group. Many times this happens when your child goes to a babysitter for the first time or enters a daycare or preschool program. "Often the preschool years mark a child's introduction to the world of peers and peer relationships. Research supports the notion that children benefit in many ways from positive peer interactions. In early childhood programs, friendships foster a sense of connection and security and build self-esteem and self-confidence, helping young children adapt more readily to the pre-school setting. Friendships provide important opportunities for children to learn and develop" (Manaster & Jobe, 2012, pp. 12, 13).

Yes, your child will learn many valuable lifetime skills as they interact with their peers. But there are times when those associations and interactions are not so positive. Have you ever received a note or a call from your child's preschool teacher informing you that your child was involved in a fight at school? It is definitely not what you want to hear as a parent and it can ruin your day. You may even be tempted to deny it or blame it all on the other child. But sooner or later you may have to admit that you must deal with it in proactive ways.

Here are some practical tips for you to help your child build positive relationships with their peers:

1. **Talk about friendship with your child.** What makes a good friend, and what can they do to be a good friend to someone else?

2. **Provide opportunities for your child to socialize with others their age.**
   The only way your child will learn important relational skills with their peer group is if they are given ample opportunities to practice. Talk to other parents and schedule regular times for your children to interact. This also gives you the opportunity to select families who share your faith values. You are also there to supervise and intervene if necessary.

3. **Teach your child to smile and greet others.**
   Role-play this with your child. This can be especially helpful if you have a shy child. Practicing with you will give them confidence. They will soon learn that if they want to have friends, they also need to be a friend.

> "What does give me happiness? Knowing that though the kids may often argue and even complain about each other, when a real challenge arises, they'll remain each other's biggest supporters"
> (Thomas, 2005, p. 133).

BULLYING

Bullying takes many forms, including teasing, verbal threats, and physical intimidation or fighting. Even parents of very young children may be faced with the issue of bullying. If you have to deal with bullies, there are two possible scenarios: (1) your child is being bullied, or (2) your child is the bully. While neither is one you want to deal with, it may actually be more challenging to accept the fact that your child *is* the bully. What are some signs that may tell you and how do you deal with each scenario? Let's look at both situations.

Is your child being bullied? Here are some signs to watch for:

- Your child loved preschool, but now doesn't want to go.

- They complain of bellyaches or headaches before being dropped off at a play date, daycare or preschool.

- They no longer want to play with a child they once liked.

- They repeatedly tell you a certain kid is "bothering," "bugging," or being mean to them.

- They suddenly become withdrawn, depressed, fearful, or clingy.

- They make derogatory remarks like "I'm a loser," "I'm stupid," or "No one likes me."

- They have unexplained boo-boos. Little ones get bumps and bruises when they play, but if your child seems to have more than a normal amount, or "forgets" the details of getting hurt, it might warrant a closer look.

> ### BASIC SOCIAL SKILLS TO TEACH YOUR CHILD
>
> - Teach them how to answer the telephone in a kind, polite, clear way.
>
> - Teach them how to greet people when they come to the door of your house—politely, respectfully, looking them in the eye, smiling, etc. Also, teach them how to greet others they meet in public or when they visit others' homes.
>
> - Teach them to value and respect others, such as the cleaning person in the office building, the gas station attendant, the grocery store clerk, the waiter or waitress at the restaurant, etc.

This first scenario is that your child is the victim and target of a bully. No parent likes to see his or her child suffer. We would much rather take the punishment ourselves then see our child hurt. So what can you do if your child is exhibiting signs that they are being bullied?

1. **Find out what's going on.** If you suspect your child is being bullied, ask your child pointed questions like, "Did someone hurt you?" or "Can you tell me exactly how this happened?" Kids this age may know that what's happening makes them feel bad, but they may not have a label for it or know how to talk about it. The more supportive you are of his feelings, the more details you'll get about what happened, how he feels about it, and how serious the situation is.

The message you want to send him is "I love you. I'm here for you. Together, we'll work on a solution."

2. **Teach your child who the trusted adults are.** Perhaps one of the greatest lessons you will teach your young child is how to speak up. Tell them who trusted adults are (mom, dad, teacher, police officers, etc.), and that the best way to stay safe is to tell a grown-up what's happening. Even if you have a young child, you are not always going to be with him or her every second of every day. Therefore, you need to demonstrate how to speak up and go over a list of adults that are trustworthy.

3. **Take action yourself.** If your child is at a babysitter's, or attends daycare or preschool, set up a meeting with the teacher or caregiver. They may be unaware of the situation—and that's not necessarily a sign of a bad sitter or teacher, just of a good bully. Keep speaking up until a solution can be found. If the bullying is going on at a playground or play date and you know the parent fairly well, you should approach them. Perhaps you can say something like, "Our children aren't getting along very well. Have you noticed?" Don't be surprised if she seems unconcerned about it. Parents are often in denial and don't always see their child's behavior as problematic. And the reality is that there may be times when the best solution is to avoid that child or find a new playground. Remember, one of your parental responsibilities is to make sure your child is safe, and you need to do what it takes for that to happen.

4. **Pray with your child.** Pray with your child about the bully. Along with your child, ask Jesus to change the bully's heart. Jesus taught us to pray for our enemies and we should teach our children the same. Remember, however, that this still does not mean putting your child in an unsafe situation! Your child needs to be assured that their safety is a priority to you.

But what if your child is the bully? Even though it may be hard to admit, you must accept the fact and deal with it. Refusing to accept it will only mean that the situation will become worse. Here are some signs to look for that may indicate your child is the one doing the bullying:

· Does your child need to feel powerful and in control?
· Is your child hot-tempered or quick to resort to aggression?
· Do they feel they do no wrong?
· Does your child show little empathy for others' feelings?
· Is your child aggressive toward adults?

In this second scenario, your child is the perpetrator. Here are some practical steps to deal with your child if he or she is the one bullying other children:

1. **Model empathy.** Teach your child that aggressive behavior is hurtful and unacceptable. If you notice acts of aggression, calmly hug your little one, make eye contact, and reiterate that it's never okay to hurt others. Instead, help them come up with an age-appropriate vocabulary so they can use non-hurtful words to express their feelings.

2. **Give positive reinforcement.** Congratulate your child for sharing, cooperating, and helping others. Parents often communicate dismay at misbehaviors, but sometimes forget to praise behaviors they like. Hugs, high fives, and

proclamations like, "I see you shared your favorite toy with Dylan—Mommy is proud of you" will make it more likely your tiny tot will continue to be nice to peers. Instead of always focusing on negative behavior, look for the positive interactions they have and point those out.

3. **Create a friend group.** Arrange supervised play dates one to three times a week, or take your child to playgrounds and organized activities where there's opportunities to interact with peers. As your child explores and interacts with peers, keep a close eye out—and intervene if you see any aggressive behavior. Being a friend is a learned skill, so give them opportunities to practice where you can closely supervise. Additionally, you can incorporate learning into your bedtime routine by reading books that reflect positive relational skills.

4. **Turn off the television.** Children love to mimic, so limit exposure to aggressive role models in the media. Replace screaming matches with heartfelt talks, and keep your easily-influenced kid away from the television set where the very behavior you are trying to eliminate is being promoted. Educational videos and public television can be great resources for age-appropriate role models, but remember how important it is to watch the program with your child and talk with them about the content. Younger children learn from aggressive behaviors or conflict scenes that are frequently portrayed in children's' programming on television.

5. **Condemn aggression.** Connect acts of aggression, such as biting or not sharing, to the hurt it causes other children—and do it right away. As a result, preschoolers will be better able to connect the dots between bullying and hurt feelings. Spanking a child to teach them not to hit his peers sends them a mixed message. Remember, you cannot stop violence with violence and you cannot stop bullying by bullying your child.

6. **Step it out.** Young preschool children need specific and easily recalled steps for being less aggressive. Develop positive ways to solve problems. When they have an issue, talk to them about alternative ways they could have handled the same problem. Use puppets, dolls, or role-play to allow your child to practice friendship formation skills. Help them create simple steps as alternatives to bullying behavior.

7. **Pray with and for your child.** When you have bedtime prayers with your child have them commit this problem to prayer. Lead them to ask Jesus to help them overcome being a bully. And remember to pray *for* your child. Jesus knows your struggles as a parent and is willing to partner with you if you ask Him to.

WRAP UP

Teaching your child to have positive relational skills is something that will last a lifetime. It is modeled at home and then carried over into the relationships they establish with their peer group. Be on the alert for signs that your child is being bullied and be willing to admit and respond appropriately if you see signs that your child is being the bully.

Don't give up. Be prayerful, persistent, consistent, and patient. Teaching your child to have positive relational skills, both in and out of the home, takes time.

5

GROUP DISCUSSION

Discuss the statement below. How does it apply to teaching your children positive relational skills? What are the specific things mentioned that you should teach your child? What are some ways you can "allow no selfishness" to live in your home?

"Parents, teach your children . . . how to conduct themselves in the home with true politeness. Educate them to show kindness and tenderness to one another. Allow no selfishness to live in the heart or find room in the home" (White, 1954, p. 143).

GROUP ACTIVITY

List some ways that you can intentionally teach your child positive relational skills:

TRY THIS AT HOME

Here are some things to try at home this week:

1. Remember to continue the "Bible Promise Project" we started in chapter one. Find a promise in the Bible that you can apply to teaching your child positive relational principles. Write it out on an index card and put it in a prominent place in your home where you can see it throughout the day. Repeat it often, memorize it, and claim it as your own. And remember to share it the next time you meet with your group members.

2. Plan a play date for your child. Observe how they interact with their peers. Do you see positive things that you can encourage and affirm? Do you observe things that need to change? Talk with your child about what it means to be a friend.

A PRAYER YOU MAY SAY

Dear Lord, help me to make my home a place that exudes your love in every relationship. Help me to be a good example to my child in the relationships I have with those around me. Keep my child safe from bullies and at the same time, help him or her to show love, kindness and respect to others. In all of our family relationships help us to reflect Your love. In Jesus' name, Amen.

REFERENCES

Manaster, H. and Jobe, M. (2012, November). "Supporting preschoolers' positive peer relationships." *Young Children*. pages 12-17.

Stopani, G. (2003). "Sibling rivalry." Retrieved from: http://www.focusonthefamily.com/parenting/building_relationships/sibling_rivalry.aspx

Thomas, G. (2005). *Devotions for Sacred Parenting*. Grand Rapids, MI: Zondervan.

White, E. G. (1954). *Child Guidance*. Hagerstown, MD: Review and Herald Publishing Association.

White, E. G. (1952). *The Adventist Home*. Hagerstown, MD: Review and Herald Publishing Association.

HELP! I'M A PARENT WEBSITE
Visit our parenting website to submit questions, find additional resources, follow a blog, sign up for a free parenting e-newsletter, and more: ***www.HelpImAParent.org***

HELP! I'M A PARENT FACEBOOK PAGE
Like us on our Facebook page: "Help! I'm a Parent" New materials are posted on a regular basis.

6. MANAGING MEDIA

SCRIPTURAL PRINCIPLE

"Finally, brethren, whatever things are true, whatever things are noble, whatever things are just, whatever things are pure, whatever things are lovely, whatever things are of good report, if there is any virtue and if there is anything praiseworthy—meditate on these things" (Philippians 4:8).

ICEBREAKER—GROUP DISCUSSION

1. REMEMBER
· As you were growing up, who made peace in your family? How did they do it?

· Who is it that makes peace in your home now? How do they do it?

2. REVIEW
· What comes to your mind when you read the list in Philippians 4:8 of our scriptural principle?

· What does that list mean to you?

3. REFLECT
· On a scale from 1 (I'm cool, calm, and collected) to 10 (I'm about to lose it), how anxious do you feel right now? Why?

· What in these words of Paul could help you relieve your anxiety?

OVERVIEW

Today's parents are dealing with issues that their own parents never had to face. The onslaught of media is a cultural change that did not enter our world until the end of the last century. However, like it or not, media is not a passing fad. Instead, it is now the fabric of our American culture. As with many things, technology has proven to be both a blessing and a curse. We have been witness to a nation's ruling party being overturned, due in part to the influence social media had upon its citizens. If it can impact a nation, it surely has an impact upon our families.

In a recent study, conducted by the Institute for Advanced Studies in Culture (2012) parents held to the belief that the family unit is in decline. To a large degree, they attributed this decline to social media. In other words, technology is blamed for the moral decline of our society at large.

> "Let parents devote the evenings to their families. Lay off care and perplexity with the labors of the day" (White, 1952, p. 192).

In this chapter of managing media we will discuss the following:

· Modeling Positive Media Choices
· Media, Media Everywhere
· Steps You May Take

MODELING POSITIVE MEDIA CHOICES

Perhaps the most important thing that you can do to get a handle on parenting in this digital world is to be a positive role model in the way that you use technology. Many young children are simply acting in ways that have been modeled for them by their parents. Too many parents operate their lives by the rule, "Do as I say, not as I do." This is no way to effectively teach your children appropriate ways to utilize social media.

As parents, you must model moderation in your own use of the television, computer, cell phone, and other forms of technology. Have you ever been guilty of instructing your child to get off of the cell phone only because you wanted it? Do you limit what your child can choose on the television because you want to watch your show instead? Do you tell your child something is inappropriate for them to watch and then watch it yourself when they are in bed?

You also need to be mindful and model the observance of laws, including laws about the use of cell phones while driving. When your little toddler becomes a teen and gets his or her driving license, they will mimic the model you have set. Do you want them texting or talking on their cell phone while driving? It is not just a matter of breaking the law—it is a matter of safety.

When it comes to being a positive role model in this area, a good rule to remember is this—if you do not want your child doing it or watching it, then neither should you. We are counseled, "The words and acts of the parents are the most potent of educating influences, for they will surely be reflected in the character and conduct of the children" (White, 1889).

GROUP DISCUSSION

- Have each group member recall the last program they watched on television.
- What values did that program teach?
- Are those the same values you want to instill in your child?

MEDIA, MEDIA EVERYWHERE

Let's get real. Your children's lives are infused with contacts, conversations, and information that, at times, seem out of your control. Most parents will readily admit that their child sees things in media that they should not be seeing, listen to things that they should not be hearing, and engaging in activities of which they do not approve. Parents have a sense that they should, in fact, be doing more, but are uncertain as to how to get a handle on social media and the digital world that has invaded their child's life. Do you often feel as if attempts to control the use of media are futile?

If you try to envelop your child in a safety net against the influence of social media, you are left with nowhere for your child to go. After all, let's face the fact that social media is all around you. There is no escaping it. So should you just admit defeat? Do you

> "A television program or an electronic game that shows someone getting hurt, hurting others, or hurting things should not be viewed by young children" (Kuzma, 2006. p. 491).

throw your hands in the air and give up? Do you lock your child in a room and try to block out all forms of media?

Dr. Kay Kuzma states, "It is not uncommon to see children of all ages glued to their joysticks for hours at a time as they slay dragons, win races, ace sporting events, and pursue enemies. For parents, trying to monitor their children's video gaming has become a nightmare. Older children are sharing inappropriate games with younger siblings; school children are copying games from their peers at school that their parents would never buy for them, and some . . . have lost touch with reality" (Kuzma, 2006, p. 493).

"Every time a man sits in front of a computer and logs onto the Internet, he creates a moral trail—will he hate sin "with a perfect hatred and seek above everything to remove and keep it out of his home," or will he allow it to infiltrate his children's abode?" (Thomas, 2005, pp. 16-17)

Because you cannot be with your child every second, and because they will grow to make their own decisions, the best thing you can do is to teach your child to manage media in responsible ways. That is your ultimate goal after all. You want them to make appropriate decisions in what they watch, listen to—and—not just because you say so, but because they have those values instilled within them.

When it comes to evaluating the use of media, Kuzma (2006) gives us three basic rules to guide in media selection:

· You may not hurt yourself.
· You may not hurt others.
· You may not hurt things.

In other words, any television show, video game, or music that portrays someone hurting themselves, hurting others, or destroying things should not be allowed in the home.

STEPS YOU MAY TAKE

A key role of parenting is to teach our children to be responsible adults. This is not a matter of control. This is a matter of living up to our God-given responsibility as parents. In so doing, we will help to assure their safety amid social media frenzy. Here are some thoughts to consider:

1. **Install Parental Control software.**
   Children should never have accounts to which you do not have complete access. Nothing should be a secret to you about their online activity. There is software available that you may install on all of your household computers that allows you to get a report of your child's online activity, and block gaming and pornography. You may want to consider Net Nanny. It is the top-rated parental control software available and it sells at a very affordable price.

2. **Set boundaries and monitor use of technology.**
   Limit time on the computer and be sure the computer is located in the main part of the house. Allowing your child to have computers in their room may limit your ability to monitor their activity and screen habits. Be prepared, because this may not be a popular move; they won't like it, but that is okay. Remember, you have a responsibility as a parent to protect your child as well as

teach them responsibility and time management.

Spend some time considering what you value as a family. Some families have decided to ban the television from their homes completely, finding the merits of television to be limited. Other families have decided to control television use and programming, again reflecting family values. This is also another area where Internet access may now be gained directly from your television. Therefore, setting boundaries and monitoring use of it is vital.

Even young children can't seem to put their cell phone down. They walk with it, eat with it, and lie in bed at night talking on it. At times they seem more attached to talking or texting on their phones than talking to family or friends in person. Texting has gotten out of control at every age and it seems as if families can no longer enjoy a family meal and eat in peace without texting or taking on the phone throughout dinner. Establish ground rules for your family, adults included, so time to talk, share, and listen are a normal part of your family's interactions. Set up no-texting times and zones and be firm on this matter. Perhaps even the adults in your home should consider a rule about putting cell phones away when they come into the home at night, or at least limit the amount of time spent on them. Otherwise, technology will control your family instead of you controlling it.

GROUP DISCUSSION

· At what age should children have a cell phone?
· What if they had an emergency?
· What about a smart phone to help them do their homework?
· What can you do if you need to get laundry or other housework done and the television, iPad, or other electronic media devises have been serving as your babysitter? What are some other options?

3. Social Media accounts
Even though Facebook and other social media sites have age restrictions, the truth of the matter is that it still depends on you, the parent, to enforce those restrictions. You may be surprised to find out that many very young children have their own social media accounts. Social media sites are not the place where our children should be engaging in conversations and chats. Do not allow it to be an option.

4. Control access to Social Media at friends' homes.
Many parents state that even if they control social media in their own home, their child is exposed to it at the home of their friends. Perhaps this is the easiest issue of all to solve. Talk to the other parents. Explain your beliefs and the guidelines that you have set as a family as it relates to time limits, what to watch, what to listen to, what to play with, etc. If it still becomes an issue, then don't allow your child to stay overnight or visit that friend's home unless you are with them. It is not harsh. Remember, you are the parent. It is your responsibility to guard what your little one puts in to their impressionable mind and this may mean that you restrict them from going to certain homes of friends.

> Disconnect in order to connect!

GROUP DISCUSSION

Should young children be allowed to spend the night at a friend's house without you? In addition to media choices, are there other things to be concerned about?

5. Model responsible behavior.
Remember, perhaps the most important thing that you can do to get a handle on parenting in this digital world is to be a positive role model in the way that you utilize media.

WRAP UP
Technology is both a blessing and a curse to today's family. It has the potential to be a wonderful contribution to your children's lives if you allow it to be a tool instead of a substitute for real relationships. Parents, you need to make sure you are setting boundaries, creating balance, and teaching responsibility. By being intentional in our ever-changing digital world, you, as a parent, may greatly reduce the likelihood of having regrets. After all, every parent wants to know they have done all they can to raise healthy, well-adjusted children—not just for life here, but more importantly, for eternity. You have a God-given responsibility to introduce your child to Jesus. There is no work more important. Everything they are exposed to should bring them closer to their Savior. Perhaps scripture should be your filter as you navigate through your digital-filled world. "Finally, brethren, whatever things are true, whatever things are noble, whatever things are just, whatever things are pure, whatever things are lovely, whatever things are of good report, if there is any virtue and if there is anything praiseworthy—meditate on these thing" (Philippians 4:8).

GROUP DISCUSSION

Discuss the statement below. How does it apply to teaching our children the importance of making positive choices in regards to media?

"To shield their children from contaminating influences, parents should instruct them in the principles of purity . . . They should surround them with influences that tend to strengthen character" (White, 1954, p. 113).

GROUP ACTIVITY

List some creative things you can do to connect as a family when you disconnect from all media:

TRY THIS AT HOME

Here are some things to try at home this week:

1. Remember to continue the "Bible Promise Project" we started in chapter one. Find a promise in the Bible that you can apply to managing media in your home. Write it out on an index card and put it in a prominent place in your home where you can see it throughout the day. Repeat it often, memorize it, and claim it as your own. And remember to share it the next time you meet with your group members.

> **BALANCE MEDIA TIME WITH THESE ACTIVITIES:**
> · Exercise
> · Reading
> · Family Time
> · Games
> · Worship

2. Take an inventory of media in your home. Look at each DVD. Does it lead your child closer to Jesus or away from Him? Note the television programming your child watches, as well as electronic games, computers, iPad, and cell phone usage, etc. Do an honest assessment. Are changes needed in any area of your home in regards to managing media?

3. Here is a challenge for you: Turn off the television in your home for the next 30 days. Spend the time reading, playing games, or enjoying other family activities you do not normally do. At the end of the 30 days, examine the impact it has had on your family.

A PRAYER YOU MAY SAY

Dear Lord, media surrounds my child every day. Wherever we go, it is there. I want my family to focus more on You and less on the television screen. I want my family to hear You more and the sounds of media less. I want You to be more appealing to them than the latest movie being released. I want them to desire and hunger to know You more than they desire the latest technological gadget. I dedicate my family to You. May everything we watch, hear, and do be to Your honor and glory and pleasing in Your sight. In Jesus' name, Amen.

REFERENCES

Institute for Advanced Studies in Culture. (2012). *Culture of American Families: Executive Report*. Charlottesville, VA: University of Virginia.

Kuzma, K, (2008). *The First 7 Years*. Nampa, ID: Pacific Press Publishing.

Thomas, G. (2005). *Devotions for Sacred Parenting*. Grand Rapids, MI: Zondervan.

White, E. G. (1954). *Child Guidance*. Hagerstown, MD: Review and Herald Publishing Association.

White, E. G. (1952). *The Adventist Home*. Hagerstown, MD: Review and Herald Publishing Association.

White, E. G. (1889). *The Health Reformer*. May 1, par. 2.

HELP! I'M A PARENT WEBSITE
Visit our parenting website to submit questions, find additional resources, follow a blog, sign up for a free parenting e-newsletter, and more: ***www.HelpImAParent.org***

HELP! I'M A PARENT FACEBOOK PAGE
Like us on our Facebook page: "Help! I'm a Parent" New materials are posted on a regular basis.

7. HEALTHY AND HAPPY

SCRIPTURAL PRINCIPLE
"Beloved, I pray that you may prosper in all things and be in health, just as your soul prospers" (3 John 1:2).

ICEBREAKER—GROUP DISCUSSION

1. REMEMBER
· What childhood illness did you have?

· Were you ever glad you were sick so you didn't have to go to school? Why?

· Were you ever upset you were sick so you couldn't go out? Why?

2. REVIEW
· Notice how Paul connects the physical with mental and spiritual (soul) health.

· Can you think of some examples of how these are related?

3. REFLECT
· What changes do I need to make so I can enjoy better physical health? Emotional health? Spiritual health?

OVERVIEW
The overall health of your family is of utmost concern. Yet all too often, you may find yourself making choices for your family that may not be the healthiest. It is easier and often cheaper to eat the unhealthy food options. It is far more appealing to skip that afternoon run and plop in front of the television after a hard day at the office. But your choices not only affect you now—you are a parent, and that means every health choice you make will also have consequences for your child. Your child eats what you eat and their exercise patterns will resemble your own. So get up and get moving!

As we delve into this topic and consider ways to teach our children to make healthy choices, we will look at the following:

· Healthy Food Choices
· Exercise
· Rest
· Mental Health
· General Health Habits

"Sleep, nature's sweet restorer, invigorates the weary body and prepares it for the next day's duties" (White,1952, p. 289).

HEALTHY FOOD CHOICES
Perhaps one of a parent's biggest challenges is how to compete with media when it comes to helping children make healthy food choices. The food-marketing experts are great when it comes to appealing to our little ones' eyes with the colorful cartoon characters that are pictured on food packaging. Take special notice in the cereal aisle the next time you go into your local grocery store. Look

at the packaging of the granola cereal and compare it to the sugary cereal. Which would appeal to you if you were a little one? Look at the colors on the packaging. Notice the graphics. It is indeed hard to compete with that!

Here are some tips to teach your child to make healthy food choices:

1. **Accept that each person is different and unique, including your child.** Let's be honest and admit that there are some foods we do not enjoy as adults. The same is true of your children. If they do not like one green vegetable, try another. After all, your goal may be to provide the nutrients that are in green vegetables. You can still achieve your goal and respect your child's individual tastes.

> "Family life is as real as it gets! Why do kids always seem to get their earaches twenty-four hours before the vacation plane is scheduled to take off? . . . let's ask God to give us gracious hearts, hearts that roll with life's punches, hearts that see humor where others see only frustration—one of the richest inheritances we can pass down" (Thomas, 2005, p. 104).

2. **Talk about food.** Toddlers are learning colors, shapes, and textures, and food is the perfect teaching tool. During conversations, discuss what a healthy food is. Start with the basics. Instead of classifying food into good and bad, teach them to think of a healthy food as something that will help them grow, get tall, become strong, play more, or run fast. Point out the various colors in vegetables and fruits. Make it a game to see how many different colors they can put on their plate.

3. **Get your child involved in food selection and meal preparation.**
   - Take your child grocery shopping and encourage them to select a vegetable or a fruit they want to try. Make it a challenge for them to select different colors from the produce section.

   - Make a habit of trying one different food or recipe every week.

   - Children like to help. Let your child wash produce, set the table, toss the salad, sprinkle cheese or spices, or anything safe for their age and ability level. Even young children can help contribute to the meal preparation. Yes, they will make messes, but it's all a part of learning.

4. **Eat at meal times only.** While it's tempting to turn the television on or feed your child when he's playing, try to avoid doing so. Avoid developing the habit of eating between meals. Try a glass of water instead. Little ones are active bundles of energy, so they may need carrot sticks or raisins to calm the hunger. Just remember to limit any snacks and, if they are needed, make them healthy.

5. **Eat meals together as a family at the table.** For younger children, bring the highchair close to the table, or remove its tray and let your child use the family table. Take the time to sit down together and reconnect as a family. Talk about the highs and lows of the day. Turn off the cell phones and the television and just enjoy each other's company.

6. **Be a positive role model.** Your actions and attitudes matter. Children who fear trying new foods have parents who do, too, and children who are picky with vegetables have parents who don't vary their vegetable intake. Children want what their parents have, so make sure you are eating healthy foods to nourish your body, too. Be aware of what you are eating. Make that carrot stick you are eating look so yummy that your little one will have to try it, too.

7. **Don't reward eating a healthy food with something that is not.** "If you don't eat your vegetables, you can't have dessert." That implies your child has to eat something that is not tasty in order to get something that is sweet and delicious. This does not encourage your child to love eating vegetables. Instead, make fruits and vegetables festive, reward with fun activities or special attention, and offer dessert occasionally, detached from eating any other food.

8. **Be patient and continue to offer a variety of foods.** When your child refuses to eat something, ask why. What caused the response: Was it taste, smell, texture, or temperature? Offer it in different cooking methods, shapes, temperatures, and offer something that looks good. If they do not like it cooked one way, try another. Don't give up. For example, they may not like cooked carrots but they may love raw carrot sticks with a healthy dip.

EXERCISE

It is far easier to get the household chores done if you sit your child down in front of the television, as opposed to encouraging them to exercise. After all, exercise usually means that you must get involved and be an active participant with them. You may live in a place where it may not be the safest thing to send them to the park to play on the playground alone, or in some cases, to even play in their own backyard. While it may be possible to get exercise in the house, it is limited at best and also denies them of breathing fresh air into their little lungs.

When most adults think about exercise, they think about working out in the gym, on a treadmill, or lifting weights. But for children, exercise means running, jumping, and playing. Children get exercise when they play hide-and-seek, while riding bikes, or when playing a game of tag.

According to the Nemours Foundation (2013), children who are physically active will:

· Have stronger muscles and bones.
· Have a leaner body, because exercise helps control body fat.
· Be less likely to become overweight.
· Decrease the risk of developing Type 2 Diabetes.
· Possibly lower blood pressure and blood cholesterol levels.
· Have a better outlook on life.

Besides enjoying the health benefits of regular exercise, children who are physically fit sleep better and are better able to handle physical and emotional challenges. The truth is, you will experience the same benefits from exercise as your children. In other words, if you exercise with your child, it is a win-win for both of you. So get up and get moving with your little one.

REST

Just as important as exercise are the times for rest. Many young children are full of energy and exercise may actually be easier to obtain than rest. It may be hard to get your little one to slow down. They seem to be one little ball of energy that always wants to be on the go.

Here are some tips to help your child relax at night and catch all the zzz's they need:

1. **Be consistent with bed times.** Put your child to bed at the same time every night; this helps their little body get into a routine.

2. **Follow a bedtime routine.** This could include taking a warm bath, getting into clean pajamas, having family worship, and saying bedtime prayers.

SLEEP, MY BABE

Sleep, my babe, and peace attend thee,
All through the night;
Guardian angels God will lend thee,
All through the night;
Soft the drowsy hours are creeping,
Hill and vale in slumber sleeping,
Mother, dear her watch is keeping,
All through the night.

God is here, thou'lt not be lonely,
All through the night;
'Tis not I who guards thee only,
All through the night.
Night's dark shades will soon be over,
Still my watchful care shall hover,
God with me His watch is keeping,
All through the night"
(Bennet, 1993, pp.743-744).

3. **Cut out all drinks that contain caffeine.** These include some sodas and other drinks, like iced tea.

4. **Don't allow any form of media in your child's room.** Research shows that children who have access to media in their rooms sleep less.

5. **Don't watch television shows or movies close to bedtime.** These can sometimes make it hard to fall asleep. Instead, do activities that calm. Play soft music or do other calming activities.

6. **Don't exercise just before going to bed.** Exercise earlier in the day. Exercise does help your child sleep better, but if the heartrate is elevated too close to bedtime, it can take longer for the child to calm down.

7. **Teach your child that their bed or crib is just for sleeping.** The bed is not for playing games or technology gadgets; it is a place to relax. Remove things that excite from the child's reach. That way, you'll train your child's little body to associate their bed with sleep.

8. **Assure them that you are close by.** Tuck your child in bed with their favorite stuffed toy or blanket. Remind them that they have been fed, they have had a drink of water, prayers have been said, and now it is time to sleep. You are not leaving and you will be there when they awaken. Remind them that Jesus and their angel are right beside them.

MENTAL HEALTH

It is often easy to overlook the possibility that even young children may have some mental health challenges. As parents, you need to be concerned about all aspects of your child's health, including their mental health.

Here are some guidelines to assist you as a parent in assuring that your child is mentally healthy:

1. **Identifying mental health disorders in children can be tricky.** Children differ from adults in that they experience many physical, mental, and emotional changes as they progress through their natural growth and development. They also are in the process of learning how to cope with, adapt, and relate to others and the world around them.

2. **Each child matures at his or her own pace.** What is considered "normal" in children falls within a wide range of behavior and abilities. This means that it is important for the parent to consider how well the child is functioning within the family circle, as well as outside of it. It is also important to understand the different ages of development, as what may be appropriate for one age may not be a sign that intervention is needed in another age bracket.

3. **Seek professional advice.** There are too many symptoms and signs to list in this manual; therefore, the most important guideline to remember is this one: If in doubt, seek help! Never be afraid to seek professional guidance. It is far better to be wrong than to not seek help and regret it later. In mental health issues, early intervention is a key. Trust your concerns! Talk to your child's physician and explain what you have noticed. They will be able to give you professional guidance.

GENERAL HEALTH HABITS
Other general health habits that your child will need to learn are things such as good hygiene. This includes good dental hygiene as well as the importance of keeping their bodies' clean, wearing clean clothes, etc.

As soon as they have that first tooth, get them their own toothbrush and teach them how to brush their teeth. You will have to do it for them at first, but soon they will want to hold that toothbrush. Let them go with you to the dentist so they will learn that the dentist is a friend.

The best way to teach them about a clean body is to make sure you give them daily baths. As they grow, they will incorporate a daily bath as a habit. You can model good hand washing habits by washing your hands before meals and after each bathroom use.

You also need to teach them the importance of wearing clean clothes every day. Show them where to put dirty laundry and let them help you fold the easy pieces like washcloths or match the socks into pairs. Talk with them about why doing laundry is important to family health.

WRAP UP
Home is the place where children learn healthy habits that will carry them throughout their lifetime. A healthy lifestyle involves making healthy choices in what we eat, the activities we participate in, the associations we have, keeping our minds healthy, and maintaining spiritual health in our relationship with Jesus.

When it comes to the spiritual health of your family, be sure to review the ideas and concepts contained in chapter three of this manual. We will also discuss mental health in the last chapter of this manual.

We have also included additional materials at the end of this chapter on "NEWSTART." Perhaps today is the day to commit to a "new start" for your family's health.

GROUP DISCUSSION

Discuss the statement below. How can health be made a "family matter"?

"Healthful living must be made a family matter" (White, 1954, p. 104).

GROUP ACTIVITY

List some creative ideas that could positively change the health of your family:

TRY THIS AT HOME
Here are some things to try at home this week:

1. Remember to continue the "Bible Promise Project" we started in chapter one. Find a promise in the Bible that you can apply to teaching your child the principles of healthy living. Write it out on an index card and put it in a prominent place in your home where you can see it throughout the day. Repeat it often, memorize it, and claim it as your own. And remember to share it the next time you meet with your group members.

2. This week, do something active outside with your child. Let them help you in planning a fun outing. And remember, you are not just taking them—you will be actively participating in whatever activity you chose.

A PRAYER YOU MAY SAY
Dear Lord, help me to model healthy choices for my family. Give me the energy to participate in daily physical activity with my child and help me to provide my family with healthy food choices. Help me to show my child a good balance in activity and in rest. Show me any areas where change is needed, so my entire family may be in optimal health in all areas. Most importantly, may I constantly reflect You, and may You be the center of my home so my family will be spiritually healthy. In Jesus' name, Amen.

REFERENCES

Bennett, W. (1993). *The Book of Virtues*. New York, NY: Simon & Schuster.

Nemours Foundation (2013). "Kids and exercise." *Kids Health*. Retrieved from: http://kidshealth.org/parent/nutrition_center/staying_fit/exercise.html#a_The_Many_Benefits_of_Exercise

Thomas, G. (2005). *Devotions for Sacred Parenting*. Grand Rapids, MI: Zondervan.

White, E. G. (1954). *Child Guidance*. Hagerstown, MD: Review and Herald Publishing Association.

White, E. G. (1952). *The Adventist Home*. Hagerstown, MD: Review and Herald Publishing Association.

HELP! I'M A PARENT WEBSITE
Visit our parenting website to submit questions, find additional resources, follow a blog, sign up for a free parenting e-newsletter, and more: *www.HelpImAParent.org*

HELP! I'M A PARENT FACEBOOK PAGE
Like us on our Facebook page: "Help! I'm a Parent" New materials are posted on a regular basis.

ADDITIONAL MATERIAL FOR
CHAPTER 7- HEALTHY AND HAPPY

Weimar Institute, located in Weimar, California, has developed an acronym to remind us of the eight principles of healthy living. The first letters of each principle spells out the word, "NEWSTART." It is an easy way to remember the keys to maintaining good health.

You may also want to visit their website for additional information and to and watch a short video clip on each of these eight principles. Perhaps it is time for a "NEWSTART" for your family's health.

1. **Nutrition**—Proper nutrition is the foundation of good health and recovery. Cooking classes, meals, and cookbooks all demonstrate the variety appeal and satisfaction of whole, plant-based vegetarian cuisine. In addition, physicians explain the issues that link nutrition with health or disease in their lectures.

2. **Exercise**—Action is a law of life. Muscle tone and strength are lost without exertion, but exercise improves the health of body, mind, and spirit multiplying vitality and health. Exercise therapy includes outdoor exercise, treadmill evaluations, and Stretchercise. The many trails through beautiful surroundings beckon you to walk, walk, walk, but indoor exercise equipment is available.

3. **Water**—Because the body is 70% water; keeping hydrated and knowing what and when to drink are essential to health. Hydrotherapy (water applied externally to the body) followed by massage enhances circulation and stimulates immune system in wonderful ways.

4. **Sunlight**—The sun is the established energy source, ordained by God, to sustain the cycle of life for plants and animals. Sunlight is supremely important for the body's metabolism and hormonal balance.

5. **Temperance**—Using good things moderately and avoiding the bad is obviously wise, yet often hard to practice. Temperance can neither be bought nor earned, but is an important gift of God, a "fruit of the Spirit" (Galatians 5:22, 23). Moderation in all things is a thread woven throughout the fabric of NEWSTART Lifestyle programs.

6. **Air**—The body's most essential resource is air. More important than food or water, proper breathing and pure air are fundamental to good health.

7. **Rest**—Restoration requires rest because sleep allows the body to renew itself. Many types of rest are important for health, but the sweetest rest follows labor. "Early to bed and early to rise" is a vital NEWSTART principle, and a healthy lifestyle makes this principle easier to maintain.

8. **Trust in Divine Power**—Directly linked to physical health (Proverbs 3:5-6), trust in God is a gift leading to right choices.

REFERENCE

Weimar Institute (2013). What is Newstart? *NEWSTART*: Weimar Institute. Retrieved from http://newstart.com/what-is-newstart/

8. RESPECT AND RESPONSIBILITY

SCRIPTURAL PRINCIPLE
"Whatever your hand finds to do, do it with your might . . ." (Ecclesiastes 9: 10).

ICEBREAKER—GROUP DISCUSSION

1. REMEMBER
· Remember the phrase, "You can't take it with you!" If you could, what one thing would you take with you when you die?

2. REVIEW
· Read Ecclesiastes 9:10. What reasons does Solomon give for doing things "with all of your might"?

· What does Solomon mean when he writes, "in the grave there is no work, no planting, no knowledge, and no wisdom?" Can you think of other biblical passages that support that idea?

3. REFLECT
· Do you feel you deserve a reward in life for your righteousness? Or maybe you might deserve a "kick-in-the-pants"? What trophy, booby prize, or punishment do you feel you deserve?

· Are there benefits to being faithful? What are they?

OVERVIEW
All of us have probably witnessed a temper tantrum. If fact, it may only be as far away as the local mall or grocery store. Sadly, it is often our own child. It is frustrating and embarrassing. It is bad enough if disrespect or disobedience happens in the confines of our home, but it is worse when it occurs in public.

All parents want their child to be respectful, both to them and to others. In addition, you want them to be responsible. Even small children may have certain responsibilities or chores, such as picking up their clothes, making their beds, or putting their toys in the toy box. Being faithful to these small, child-like responsibilities will teach big lessons later in life.

As we consider ways you can teach your child to be respectful and responsible, we will consider the following:

· Discipline vs. Punishment
· Teaching Respect
· Teaching Responsibility

> "If we would have our children practice kindness, courtesy, and love, we ourselves must set them the example" (White, 1952, p. 421).

DISCIPLINE VS. PUNISHMENT
Did you know that there is a difference between discipline and punishment? Do you know what that difference is? Valya Telep (2009) explains it this way: "Effective discipline helps children learn to control their behavior so that they act according to their ideas of what is right and wrong,

not because they fear punishment. For example, they are honest because they think it is wrong to be dishonest, not because they are afraid of getting caught." On the other hand, "the purpose of punishment is to stop a child from doing what you don't want—and using a painful or unpleasant method to stop him" (p. 2).

Punishment is characterized by the tendency to be harsh and abusive. It is important to be honest with yourself. The following is a list of abusive behavior toward children:

> "When children willfully make wrong choices, lead them gently to the cross to ask Jesus for forgiveness and for power to do what is right" (Kuzma, 2006, p. 128).

- Any physical punishment that is harsh and unreasonably painful, even though it may have resulted in changed behavior.

- Any impulsive, irrational reaction that is inflicted merely as an appeasement for parental anger.

- Any treatment of children that makes them feel embarrassed or belittled, whether it is in private or in public.

- Any words that cut down children's self-respect or diminish the positive feelings they have about themselves.

- Any behavior that causes children to feel alienated from their family or from God.

As you reviewed the list above, did you notice any abusive behaviors of which you have been guilty? If so, seek forgiveness and help immediately. Ask God to help you be a God-led parent. As adults, we sin every day. Yet God, our Father, loves us and forgives us. He never deals with us in an abusive or harsh manner. He always welcomes us in His arms of love. In like manner, we should deal with our children by practicing beneficial discipline rather than harsh punishment.

GROUP ACTIVITY

"There is no fear in love; but perfect love casts out fear, because fear involves torment. But he who fears has not been made perfect in love" (1 John 4:18).

1. Read the text above together as a group.

2. Share your thoughts with each other on the meaning for parents.

3. Individually rewrite the text in your own words to reflect the relationship God wants you to have with your child. Share it with your group.

The ultimate purpose of discipline is to help your child change their behavior; isn't that your goal as a parent? We want to have our children alter their behavior and understand the difference between right and wrong. You want to equip them with the tools to make good choices next time, and this is the purpose of discipline. You want to teach your child to be self-disciplined, to make good moral choices, and to internalize values.

If the ultimate goal of discipline is to teach your children to be self-disciplined and willingly obedient, how is this accomplished? Here are some tips to keep in mind:

- Spend enjoyable quality time with them.
- Expect them to obey.
- Make sure your children know that you mean what you say.
- Be consistent.
- Give your child a choice when possible.
- If married, keep a united front.
- Err on the side of mercy, rather than severity.
- Be the kind of person you want your child to be.
- Seek God's guidance.

COMMANDMENTS FOR THE HOME
Write the following commandments on the doorposts of your home.
- For Children: "Honor your father and your mother" (Exodus 20:12).

- For Parents: "Do not provoke your children" (Colossians 3:21).

- For all: "Esteem others better than yourselves" (Philippians 2:3), (Kuzma, 2006. p. 132).

TEACHING RESPECT
Respect means honoring other people and treating them with care, courtesy, and kindness. While respect includes good manners, the core of the behavior goes deeper than mere politeness. Respect stems from the belief that other people have as much worth and dignity as you, and that harming others or their property is inherently wrong. Children usually learn to be respectful of rules at home and at school, to not make fun of friends, and to use polite speech. But learning it and making it a part of daily practice can be two different things.

CHORES FOR ALL
Encourage participation in household chores by all the members of the family. Everyone can contribute to the household duties, according to their age, size, and ability.

The challenge of today is that respectful behavior seems to have fallen by the wayside in many of the television shows your child may watch. Take note the next time you sit with your child in front of the television. Listen to the way that children on some of the most popular television shows interact with the adults. Disrespect is the norm, and misbehavior of children is laughed at. This puts even more responsibility on you, the parent, to teach your child the importance of respecting and valuing everyone.

Dr. Robyn J.A. Silverman (2008) offers these parenting tips for teaching respect and curbing disrespect:

1. **Model it:** If you want them to do it, you have to do it, too.

2. **Expect it:** When your expectations are reasonably high, children rise to the occasion.

3. **Teach it:** Give children the tools they need to show you respect. Be intentional about teaching it. Role-play various situations with them using puppets or dolls. If they are using words that show disrespect or using non-verbal language that shows the same, teach them different words to use and different ways to respond.

4. **Praise it:** When you see or hear your children using respectful language and making respectful choices, recognize it and praise them for making positive, respectful decisions.

"I'd like to suggest a motto for Christian family life: 'God is in the room'. Think of how differently we might treat our children in those frustrating moments if we responded to them with the knowledge that God is in the room. If we truly believed that the God who designed them and who is passionate about their welfare was literally looking over our shoulders, might we be a little more patient, a little more understanding? Tell it to yourself, every morning, every noontime, every evening: God is in the room. Tell it to each other, every time you're tempted to yell, or criticize, or ridicule, or even ignore each other: God is in the room. Tell it to your children, throughout the day: God is in the room. Let's keep telling it to ourselves and to each other until we practice it and live it, until we live and breathe with the blessed remembrance: 'God is in the room'. 'God is in the room' " (Thomas, 2005, pp. 9-10).

5. **Discuss it:** Pick out times when you see other children using respectful or disrespectful language or behavior and discuss with it your children. Use it as teachable moments for your child.

6. **Address it:** Don't just let things slide! Be sure to notice when respectful behavior is being exhibited and make sure to call them on disrespectful behavior! And, if you notice disrespect being modeled by a character on television, TURN IT OFF! Do not allow them to watch that show. Media is a powerful teaching tool and if they are watching anything that is modeling disrespect, you must not allow it. You cannot negate what you say by what you allow them to watch.

7. **Understand it:** Your children are growing and learning. Sometimes word choice and behavioral decisions are made because they do not have the correct words or behavior to relay, "I'm tired," "I'm frustrated," or "I'm angry."

8. **Reinforce it:** A great place to reinforce the importance of being respectful is at family worships. Help your child memorize a Bible verse that speaks of how much Jesus values and loves us. In the same way we should show love and respect to all of His creation.

9. **Reward it:** Respectful behavior should be something that children want to do without overindulgent rewards. However, it is good to associate respectful behavior with intangible rewards such as praise, recognition, or extra responsibility and privileges. Be as quick to affirm as you are to correct.

Did you happen to notice the first step above? As with most of the principles we discuss in this series, teaching respect starts with you being respectful. Dr. Kay Kuzma (2006, pp. 131-132) suggests the following guidelines as to how parents can model respect:

· Be consistent and follow through on what you say.

· Keep your promises.

· When you want compliance, get down on your child's level, look into their eyes, hold their hands gently, and speak clearly so they can understand.

· Be fair and reasonable.

· Be cool, calm, and collected when correcting, taking care not to embarrass your child.

· Honor each child's individual abilities, interests, and needs.

· Guard your child's reputation; never criticize them in public.

· Be courteous and respectful to your spouse, friends, and neighbors.

· Insist that all members of the family be respectful to each other.

· Respect your child's property rights and their need for privacy.

· Consider how you would like to be treated if you were a child and respond accordingly.

· Write the following commandments on the doorposts of your home.

  · For Children—"Honor your father and your mother" (Exodus 20:12).

  · For Parents—"Do not provoke your children" (Colossians 3:21).

  · For all—"Esteem others better than yourselves" (Philippians 2:3).

· Reverence God and show respect to other authorities.

TEACHING RESPONSIBILITY

Even young children need to be taught to be responsible. For them it may mean picking up their clothes, coming to dinner when called, helping mom set the table, etc. Many parents may resort to yelling, screaming or demanding, all of which yield no lasting result. What's a parent to do?

Helping children understand that the choices they make in life come with a natural consequence can be a very valuable lesson. Telep (2009) reminds us that the use of natural consequences is a great way to teach responsibility. Remember that giving a child a choice and allowing him or her to experience the consequences is one of the best ways children learn. Consequences can be used to get children to school on time, to meals on time, and to take responsibility for chores. The child learns that if he or she doesn't pick up the toys, there's no moving onto the next activity; if he or she doesn't pick up the clothes and place them in the laundry basket, they will not be washed; if he or she does not come when called to the dinner table, dessert will be missed. In each case, the consequence is a natural result of a choice the child made.

Think about these ideas:

· Using consequences as a disciplinary method helps children learn to take responsibility for their own behavior.

· Consequences must be logically related to the misbehavior. They cannot be arbitrary.

· The child must see the relationship between his misbehavior and the consequences or it will not work.

· The child must know that the consequences are a result of their own choice.

· Use consequences in a firm, kind, and friendly manner.

· Be consistent.

"Using consequences takes practice. It is not easy to use consequences as a way to discipline children. It is hard work to think of consequences that really are logical. And it requires lots of patience! Sometimes it takes several weeks to get results. Parents are so used to telling children what to do that it is very difficult to sit back and let the child experience the consequences of his actions. The effort is well worth it, however, because you are sending a powerful message to the child that says, 'you are capable of thinking for yourself'" (Telep, 2009. pp. 5, 6).

WRAP UP
The ultimate goal of parenting is to raise your child to make wise decisions and be self-governing. It will serve no lasting goal if their behavior is only based on fear of punishment. They need to learn that every choice they make in life will have natural consequences—whether good or bad. They need to take ownership of their own choices and learn to lean on God to guide and lead them in those choices.

GROUP DISCUSSION

Discuss the statement below. How does this say you are to discipline your children? Who does it mention should be involved in the teaching, training and educating of your little ones?

"The requirements of the parents should always be reasonable; kindness should be expressed, not by foolish indulgence, but by wise direction. Parents are to teach their children pleasantly, without scolding or faultfinding, seeking to bind the hearts of the little ones to them by silken cords of love. Let all, fathers and mothers, teachers, elder brothers and sisters, become an educating force to strengthen every spiritual interest, and to bring into the home and the school life a wholesome atmosphere, which will help the younger children to grow up in the nurture and admonition of the Lord" (White, 1954, p. 86).

GROUP ACTIVITY

List some behavioral challenges of younger children. Then list some ways that natural consequences could be used to help alter their behavior:

TRY THIS AT HOME
Here are some things to try at home this week:

1. Remember to continue the "Bible Promise Project" we started in chapter one. Find a promise in the Bible that you can apply to teaching your child to be respectful and responsible. Write it out on an index card and put it in a prominent place in your home where you can see it throughout the day. Repeat it often, memorize it, and claim it as your own. And remember to share it the next time you meet with your group members.

2. Take note of the television shows your child is watching this week. Do all the interactions model behaviors you want your child to emulate? Is change needed?

A PRAYER YOU MAY SAY
Dear Lord, help me to show my child the importance of respecting and valuing all of Your creation. It makes no difference if plant, animal, or another fellow being. You created all, and all deserve the same love and respect that You give it. Help me to model the kindness and respect that I want them to have. Help me to also teach them the importance of being responsible and keeping their word. In the same way help me to be faithful to my duties. Once again, I dedicate my family to You. In Jesus' name, Amen.

REFERENCES

Bennett, W. (1993). *The Book of Virtues*. New York, NY: Simon & Shuster.

Kuzma, K, (2008). *The First 7 Years*. Nampa, Idaho: Pacific Press Publishing.

Silverman, R. (April 12, 2008). "10 Tips on Teaching Respect to Children: You can't get it if you don't give it!" *Dr. Robyn Silverman*. Retrieved from : http://www.drrobynsilverman.com/parenting-tips/10-tips-on-teaching-respect-to-children-you-cant-get-it-if-you-dont-give-it/

Telep, V. (2009, May). "Discipline for young children, Lesson 2: Discipline and Punishment: What is the difference?" *Virginia Cooperative Extention*. Petersburg, VA: Virginia State University. Publication 350-111. Retrieved from http://pubs.ext.vt.edu/350/350-111/350-111.html

Thomas, G. (2005). *Devotions for Sacred Parenting*. Grand Rapids, MI: Zondervan.

White, E. G. (1954). *Child Guidance*. Hagerstown, MD: Review and Herald Publishing Association.

White, E. G. (1952). *The Adventist Home*. Hagerstown, MD: Review and Herald Publishing Association.

HELP! I'M A PARENT WEBSITE
Visit our parenting website to submit questions, find additional resources, follow a blog, sign up for a free parenting e-newsletter, and more: ***www.HelpImAParent.org***

HELP! I'M A PARENT FACEBOOK PAGE
Like us on our Facebook page: "Help! I'm a Parent" New materials are posted on a regular basis.

9. TIME, TALENTS, AND TREASURES

SCRIPTURAL PRINCIPLE
"For where your treasure is, there your heart will be also" (Matthew 6:21).

ICEBREAKER—GROUP DISCUSSION

1. REMEMBER
· When you were a teenager, what did your parents think of the clothes you wore? Did they think they were strange, immodest, or ragged?

· What is your favorite clothing store? Where do you find the best bargains?

2. REVIEW
· When it comes to your treasure (finances), Jesus reminds us in Matthew 6:21 that our treasures are where our hearts are. What do you think He meant by that?

· What is the relationship between our treasure and our heart? Between the heart and the eye? Between the eye and the body?

· How does your choice of treasure affect your life?

3. REFLECT
· Think about this past week; is your bank (treasure) on earth or in heaven? What would you need to do to change where your account is?

· Why worry when you can pray? What causes you to worry the most? What signs would tell you that you're worrying too much?

OVERVIEW
Merriam Webster (2013) defines stewardship as "the careful and responsible management of something entrusted to one's care." In this chapter we will discuss the management of time, talents, and treasures. When asked, most people will tell you that they have no time, no talents, and need more treasures. However, reality is that we all have the same amount of time, God has given everyone of us talents, and most of us have too much "stuff."

Time management, the cultivation of talents, and the wise use of material possessions are some of the greatest lessons that you, as a parent, will teach to your children. As we delve into the topic of stewardship we will discuss the following topics:

· Time
· Talents
· Treasures
· Tithing

> "From a worldly point of view, money is power; but from the Christian standpoint, love is power" (White, 1952, p. 195).

TIME
Our great, great, grandparents would perhaps laugh at us today if they were to hear us complain about the lack of time. Think about it! Most of us do not have to go out in the garden and plow the fields, harvest the vegetables, milk the

cow, sew our clothes, dry our laundry on the clothes line, or make our own soap. They would be amazed at all of the time-saving devices we have available to us in today's world.

Think about it. We have ready-made dinners that can be popped in the microwave and ready in a few minutes. We have automatic clothes washers, dryers and dishwashers. And we don't even have to go to shopping at all because we can order whatever we want online and have it delivered to our door. Yet we have no time!

The reality is that busyness is a challenge today. That challenge only increases when you are a parent and have the added responsibility of caring for a little one. The available hours seem to shrink even more. There seems to be too much to do in too little time. And yet, it is important to teach your toddler good time management. If they do not learn it when they are small, you can count on them having a struggle with being on time for college classes or being on time every morning at their jobs when they are adults.

So how do you teach that little toddler the value of time? How do you teach them to make good choices in the way they spend the 24 hours in every day? Here are some ways to teach your young child to manage their time wisely:

1. **As a parent, do you have good time management skills?** Show your child by your actions that keeping your commitments and being at your appointments on time are important to you. This includes being at your own job or doctor appointments. Your child will develop time management skills similar to your own. If you do not value being on time, neither will your child.

2. **Help your child meet his/her scheduled appointments on time.** This will teach your child that when something has a start time, it is appropriate to turn up just before that time. This applies to being at the babysitter's, preschool, or Sabbath School on time.

3. **Give your child a kitchen timer or an alarm clock.** You may teach the value of time by giving your child an alarm clock or a simple kitchen timer. Set the kitchen timer for tasks such as cleaning their room. A timer is also a great devise to use for bedtimes. For example, when it is 15 minutes before bedtime, you can set the timer. As they see the minutes tick by, they will soon understand how long that is. But stick to the times you set! As they grow, you may want to give them an alarm clock, teach them how to set it, and allow them to get themselves up at the same time every morning. This will teach them time management skills and how to tell time.

4. **Have a regular morning and evening routine.** These should cover the important basics such as teeth brushing, showering, and homework. Once again, a regular schedule with routines will teach them time management skills.

5. **Allow your child to have increased choices.** You child will learn responsibility and time management by having more control over their own time as they get older. Start simple and increase choices as they show responsibility with time.

GROUP ACTIVITY

Scripture reminds us that there is a time for everything.

Read Ecclesiastes 3:1-8.

Together, make a list of all the things for which "there is a time," according to Solomon. How does this apply to parenting?

TALENTS

Have you ever heard someone say, "I have no talent at all?" This is a common statement that is simply not true. God has given every one of us a talent. The challenge and reward comes when we discover that talent and develop it to use for His glory.

Even in very young children, parents can begin to see certain talents or leanings take shape. Perhaps they are very gifted at sports, singing, drawing, etc. And when you see that strong willed child stomping their little feet perhaps you are witnessing a budding attorney. Perhaps your child is good in math; you could be raising an accountant or an engineer.

We still remember our little girl as a toddler as she became absorbed in books that had to do with the human body. She liked learning about the skeletal system and blood vessels. Every trip to the local library would result in a bag of new books that she had selected on the topic. She would also select videos to watch that showed how all of the systems of our body worked together. We talked about what a great Creator God we had, who thought of even the tiniest details. When she was in kindergarten, she dressed for career day in a doctor's coat and wore a stethoscope around her neck. As she grew, this interest continued and today she is a physician. Yes, that interest and gift was there from early childhood, and it was our job as parents to provide resources and opportunities for our little girl to develop those interests and gifts God had given her.

Here are some practical steps to help you discover and nurture your child's God-given abilities (Burns, 2011):

1. **Discover your child's God-given talents by listening and observing.** Giving your child opportunities to participate in different activities will help you uncover and develop their talents. Maybe it's a field trip to the local museum that will open your child's eyes to a new activity they'd enjoy pursuing. Notice

the books that they select on their own at the library or bookstore. Do they seem to follow a certain theme?

2. **Encourage, but don't push.** Helping your children discover their talents can be rewarding, but remember, they may resent it if you push too hard. While some children who are talented in music may aspire to be concert pianists, others may just enjoy playing music. Hour after hour of piano practice to children who have other interests may only discourage them. Nurture their individual, God-given talents and you will find that they naturally have a desire to learn in that area.

> "Let's be careful we don't value a spotless floor over a positive, nurturing, and encouraging relationship with our kids; that we don't make them feel guilty for the impossibility of living in a house without leaving some kind of mess behind. The day will come when they won't soil the floor, touch the walls, or create additional laundry—and I suspect we'll miss the good old days when the yard showed the effects of heavy traffic and the house revealed the presence of children" (Thomas, 2005, p. 31).

3. **Provide resources.** Check out resources in your community to help develop your child's talent. Visit museums, or find books and videos. Chat with neighbors or coworkers who may also be gifted in the same area as your child and may be willing to be a positive adult mentor.

TREASURES

One need only open a child's toy box or closet to discover that there is no shortage of "treasures" for the average child today. The biggest challenge is in deciding which toy to play with. And regardless of how many toys your child may have, it seems they always want more. Television informs them of the latest and greatest toy or gadget. Parents often dread trips to the mall because of the begging they know will certainly ensue. It seems as if there is no such thing as "delayed gratification" for today's child. They want it all and they want it now!

A psychological experiment known as "the marshmallow test" (University of Pennsylvania, 2013) has captured the public's imagination as a marker of self control and even as a predictor of future success in children. This was a test that measured self-control in children, as well as their ability to practice delayed gratification.

In the classic marshmallow test, researchers gave children a choice between one or two marshmallows. Of course the child would prefer two marshmallows to one any day. Then the experimenter tells the child that they need to leave the room for "a little while." One marshmallow is placed on the table in front of the child. The child is told that, if they can hold off eating that one marshmallow, they can have the two marshmallows when he returns. With the child left alone in the room, hidden cameras tracked how long (or if) they were able to resist the temptation. Most of the children tested tried to wait, but ended up caving within a few minutes.

Tracking the children over time, researchers concluded that the ability to hold out in this seemingly trivial exercise had real and profound consequences. As they matured and became adults, the kids who had shown the ability to wait got better grades, were healthier, enjoyed greater professional success, and proved better at staying in relationships even decades after they took the test. They were, in short, better at life. The simple marshmallow test changed the way educators and psychologists thought about success. The lesson learned was that it's not just intelligence that matters, but self-control, patience, and being able to tame one's impulses through delayed gratification.

The children's responses seem illogical to us as adults. After all, why wouldn't you wait in order to get a bigger reward? Delayed gratification is something we all struggle with from time to time. But let's be honest—Even as adults, when we want it, we want it now!

The question this raises is truly one for us, as parents, in teaching Christian stewardship principles to our children. Teaching is best taught by modeling the same behavior that we want our children to emulate. Is it a common practice in our homes to lay before God all of our wants and needs? Do our children see us, as parents, satisfying all of our heart's desires, or do they see us kneeling before God, asking Him to help us get our priorities in line with His will for our lives?

Consider this important counsel, "Teach your children from the cradle to practice self-denial and self-control. Bring them up to have sound constitutions and good morals. Impress upon their tender minds the truth that God does not design that we shall live for present gratification merely, but for our ultimate good. These lessons will be as seed sown in fertile soil, and they will bear fruit that will make your hearts glad" (White, 1954, p. 113). These powerful words, written many years ago, still ring true today. The lessons we teach our children from the cradle will bear fruit throughout their entire lifetime, and indeed, into eternity.

GROUP DISCUSSION

Discuss the statement below. Do you agree with it? What do you think are God's plans for our children?

"God has much bigger plans for our children than merely indulging them" (Kimmel, 2006, p. 3).

If, as indicated by research and divine counsel, delayed gratification or self-control influences so many aspects of our children's future, how can we, as parents, teach this important life skill to our children? How do you teach them that more "stuff" does not bring true happiness?

1. **Be a Positive Christian Role Model:** This is the most important way to teach self-control and delayed gratification. How do we handle our own money? Do we have a budget? A savings account? Do our children witness us saving to buy purchases? Do they hear us praying for wisdom regarding our financial decisions? After all, this really is an issue of practicing Christian stewardship principles.

2. **Teach Waiting:** Many parents have their child save only a portion of the money needed to purchase a "want." They then take the rest of the needed money out of their own wallets to "make up the difference." Instead, teach your child(ren) to save their own money for the desired object. You will be amazed at how many times they decide not to buy it as soon as they have the money saved.

3. **Teach the Value of a Penny:** Look for opportunities to reinforce the point that by them having spent money on seemingly small, immediate gratifications (ice cream, soda, arcade games), they are not in a position to buy something they really want. The purchase may have only seemed like pennies at the moment, but those pennies add up. Help them keep track of the little things they buy and show them how those pennies they spent add up to dollars that could have been saved.

4. **Teach Consequences:** When they buy something, make a note to ask them a week (for smaller children) or a month later if they think it was a smart choice. Was it worth their money? What if you placed that item (or items) on the table in front of the child, along with the cash that equaled the purchase price? Which would they pick today? You may be surprised to see how many children admit that they made a poor decision and would rather have the money in their pockets.

5. **Teach Saving:** Set up a savings account for them. Sit down and go over the account with them so that they can see the progress they are making month after month and year after year. This is an opportunity to teach valuable lessons about compound interest and seeing how saving is built up over time. This can be done for small children. Most banks have savings plans that encourage little ones to learn the importance of saving.

TITHING

Throughout this series we have looked at the importance of modeling. When I was a little girl I remember sitting at the table with my mother and watching her calculate her tithe, write the check, and take it to church on Sabbath mornings. Today's children do not see that. Most parents give their tithe and offerings to their local church via online giving. This may be the easiest thing to do, but it also robs your child of important modeling. It is harder for them to grasp the concepts involved in money, giving, offerings, tithing, etc. when money is not something they see, touch, and hold. As a result, we encourage you to consider ways you can teach your child the value of money by having them see, touch, count, and manage it as often as possible and to witness you doing the same. If you chose to tithe online, take the opportunity to sit your child on your lap and show them what you are doing and explain why.

As soon as a child can count to ten, you can begin to teach them the concept of tithing. Do not wait until they become a teenager. Start with pennies now and teach them the joy of giving. If they do not learn with their pennies now, they will not want to share their dollars tomorrow.

The concept of tithing ten percent is really quite easy to teach to your toddler. Place ten pennies before your little one. Have them touch each penny and count aloud: "1, 2, 3 . . .10." Prepare three envelopes. Label them as follows:

· For Jesus
· To Save
· To Spend

Very simply, explain to your child that one-tenth belongs to Jesus. It will be used to help other boys and girls learn about Him so that He can be their best friend too. Have them count their pennies again. Then show them that Jesus asks for only one of their pennies. Let them place that one penny in the envelope that is marked "for Jesus." Most children will be amazed that Jesus only asks for one of their pennies and offer to put in more. Later you can help them fill out their own tithe envelope and allow your child to take their envelope to church and place it in the offering plate themselves.

Then pick up the next envelope that is labeled "to save." Explain to them that if there is something they want, they must save their pennies for it (refer to the principle of delayed gratification explained above). Have them count their pennies again: "1, 2, 3 . . . 9." They have nine pennies left. So, out of the nine pennies, how many do they want to save? Let them place those pennies in that envelope.

The remaining envelope, "to spend," is for the remainder of their pennies. This amount is for them to use at their own discretion. Allow them to make the decision. Keep track of how they spend it. Review their spending habits with them. Ask them if their choice was a wise decision or if they should have saved longer for something bigger. They will learn very quickly that those pennies add up week by week.

As your little one grows, those pennies become dimes and the dimes become dollars. Those ten pennies and three envelopes will teach valuable life lessons.

WRAP UP
We all have the same 24 hours in a day. Yet how you use those hours depend on the choices you make. Your child will need proper role modeling and guidance in order to develop good time management skills.

God has blessed every one of you and your children with varied talents. Keep your eyes open and look for those interests and gifts He has placed in your child. Provide the resources and opportunities your child needs to develop those gifts to their full potential. Then, help them look for avenues to use those gifts to glorify God.

A treasure to a young child includes such things as their toys and clothes. Teach them to care for them. Also, regardless of how few pennies they may have, as soon as they are able to count to ten, teach them the concept of tithing.

God has blessed us with so much. The concept of stewardship really means to take care of all He has entrusted to us.

GROUP DISCUSSION

Discuss each of the statements below. How do they each apply to teaching your children the stewardship principles of time, talents, and treasures? How is time "squandered"? How can talents be improved? How do you teach your child to be "caretakers" of their treasures?

Time—"The value of time is beyond computation. Time squandered can never be recovered . . . The improvement of wasted moments is a treasure" (White, 1954, p. 123).

Talents—"God's plan of life has a place for every human being. Each is to improve his talents to the utmost; and faithfulness in doing this, be the gifts few or many . . ." (White, 1954, p. 293).

Treasures—"If they are not educated to be caretaking, they will grow up with unlovely, destructive traits of character" (White, 1954, p. 101).

GROUP ACTIVITY

Individually list the talents of each one in your family. Then, write one way those talents may be used this week to glorify God. Share with the group.

TRY THIS AT HOME
Here are some things to try at home this week:

1. Remember to continue the "Bible Promise Project" we started in chapter one. Find a promise in the Bible that you can apply to teaching your child the stewardship principles of using their time, talents, and treasures in ways to glorify God. Write it out on an index card and put it in a prominent place in your home where you can see it throughout the day. Repeat it often, memorize it, and claim it as your own. And remember to share it the next time you meet with your group members.

2. Review the list contained in the "Treasures" section of this chapter. Are there things in that list you can incorporate in your home this week?

A PRAYER YOU MAY SAY
Dear Lord, help me to teach my child how to make wise use of their time. Help me

to guide them as they learn to identify and develop the gifts and talents You have given to them. Help me to teach them that true treasures do not lie in "stuff," but that the real treasure is in knowing You. In Jesus' name, Amen.

REFERENCES

Burns, A. (2011, September 20). "Help Your Child Discover Her Talents." Retrieved from: http://www.sheknows.com/parenting/articles/836807/helping-your-child-discover-their-talents

Kimmel, T. (2006). *Raising Kids for True Greatness*. Nashville, TN: Thomas Nelson.

Merriam-Webster Web. (n.d.). *Merriam-Webster.com*. (Oct. 2013). Retrieved from: http://www.merriam-webster.com/dictionary/stewardship

Thomas, G. (2005). *Devotions for Sacred Parenting*. Grand Rapids, MI: Zondervan.

University of Pennsylvania. (2013, March 30). "Delaying Gratification, Improving Self Control, And The Marshmallow Test." *Medical News Today*. Retrieved from http://www.medicalnewstoday.com/releases/258323.php.

White, E. G. (1954). *Child Guidance*. Hagerstown, MD: Review and Herald Publishing Association.

White, E. G. (1952). *The Adventist Home*. Hagerstown, MD: Review and Herald Publishing Association.

HELP! I'M A PARENT WEBSITE
Visit our parenting website to submit questions, find additional resources, follow a blog, sign up for a free parenting e-newsletter, and more: ***www.HelpImAParent.org***

HELP! I'M A PARENT FACEBOOK PAGE
Like us on our Facebook page: "Help! I'm a Parent" New materials are posted on a regular basis.

10. PARENTING PARTNERS

SCRIPTURAL PRINCIPLE

"Listen to counsel and receive instruction, that you may be wise in your latter days" (Proverbs 19:20).

ICEBREAKER—GROUP DISCUSSION

1. REMEMBER

· Do you recall a time as a child, youth, or adult when you thought you could do something on your own but couldn't? Who helped you?

· Do you recall a very useful piece of parenting advice that has helped you since you received it? What was it?

2. REVIEW

· Chapter 19 of Proverbs includes a series of instructional sayings. Make a list of the principles for parents found in this chapter. Are there any other teachings you find practical for you and your personal experience?

3. REFLECT

· Do you have "counselors," that is, people you trust for counsel and advice? If not, what steps do you need to take to surround yourself with trusted counselors?

OVERVIEW

Parenting is both the most rewarding and the most challenging task of your life. The time will come when you will need help. Consider this statement, "All families need support, assistance, and resources to thrive. Parents function best when they have a dependable network of people they can turn to for advice and concrete help with child rearing. Most families can rely on relatives, friends, and neighbors to provide the backbone of their family support network. All families benefit from access to a community system of high quality services that strengthen and support them in their parenting and nurturing roles . . ." (*Kids Count*, 2005, p.1).

Yes, there are times when we all need help. Admitting that is not a sign of weakness. Rather, it is a sign of strength. The questions become who, when, and where? Who do you turn to for help? Sometimes all the help you need is just a phone call away. But sometimes Mom, Auntie, or the pastor does not have the skills to deal with your specific needs, or the needs of your child. When do you admit that you need professional help? And where do you go to find Biblical based counseling?

In this chapter we will look at the following:

· Partnering with God
· Partnering with Family and Friends
· Partnering with the Faith Community/Church
· Partnering with a Professional

> "Your compassionate Redeemer is watching you with love and sympathy, ready to hear your prayers and to render you the assistance which you need" (White, 1952, p. 204).

PARTNERING WITH GOD

Your first and primary parenting partner should be Jesus Christ. The reality is, however, that so much time is spent in fretting and worrying that you forget He is waiting to help you with the biggest of your parenting challenges. He is only waiting for you to seek His help.

"You are the right person for the job, because God himself has assigned you the task. And he is committed to seeing you through" (Thomas, 2005, p. 14).

You are a loving caregiver to this child who is on loan to you for such a short time in their life. You have been given a few short years to help to shape and mold them into the person God wants them to be. The good news is that you aren't parenting alone—you are co-parenting with God. Isn't that an awesome thought? Give thanks to God, who promises to guide, inspire, nurture, and sustain you as you tend to the bodies and minds of your little ones.

Realize that your children belong to God and that He has allowed you to walk side by side with Him in raising them. What a blessing to help them blossom into their own unique selves! It sure makes changing diapers, washing bottles, chasing balls, washing dirty little faces, and doing yet another load of laundry a bit less tedious when you consider the awesome privilege God has given you. He has allowed you to be a partner with him in the creation of life. And He also wants to be a partner in their upbringing.

It's easy to forget that we're not CEO of this operation. The Creator, who knit our children together in the womb (Ps. 139:13) and has numbered the very hairs on their heads (Matt. 10:30), holds the blueprint for their lives. That's fine in theory of course, but how do you fully trust God when your child becomes dangerously sick, or when he makes a choice with painful consequences? What happens when you doubt your parenting ability, or when your imagination reminds you of everything that could go wrong?

God never said parenting would be easy. But He did say that He "will never leave" us or "forsake" us (Heb. 13:5). And He reminds us that we "can do all things through Him who strengthens us" (Phil. 4:13). We also know that He "has not given us a spirit of fear, but of power, love, and a sound mind" (2 Tim. 1:7). These are promises we can hold onto, no matter what our struggle may be. Trust God. He wants to partner with you as you raise your child. Talk to Him about your joys and sorrows as a parent. Claim those beautiful promises in the Bible and cling to them. God is your very best parenting partner. After all, as much as you love your little bundle of joy, God loves them even more!

PARTNERING WITH FAMILY AND FRIENDS

There are times when a call to Mom or Grandma may be just what you need as a parent. They may have just the answer you need. Your mom or dad may have experienced similar issues with you, and sometimes just listening and following their advice is all that is needed to get you over a hurdle. You can also partner with family members for childcare in order to get away for an evening or a weekend. If you are married, remember the concepts that we shared in chapter two about the importance of spending quality time together as a couple and nurturing the marriage relationship.

A family member such as a parent or sibling who is willing to spend time with your child can be very helpful and has the added bonus of widening your child's sense of family and belonging. Children know when they are with a family member. It broadens and strengthens the sense of connection while also providing a sense of individual heritage and history. Family members tell stories. They paint emotional pictures with their words that children internalize as part of themselves. When a family member helps with babysitting, goes on outings with you, or simply comes to the house to give you some adult conversation or a brief respite, you get some relief while your child extends their sense of who they are. It is a win-win situation for both you and your child.

Friends can also give you the benefit of their own experience in solving problems that you find yourself facing on a day-to-day basis. If you like the parenting styles of your friends, they can be a great resource to give you additional parenting advice on specific issues. Friends also may have already worked through a problem you are facing and can give advice or lead you in the right direction to get additional help.

PARTNERING WITH THE FAITH COMMUNITY/CHURCH

Partnering with the faith community and church members may be a good option at times. After all, they share the same faith values as you do. Seek others in the church to be prayer partners. Share specific challenges you are facing and ask them to lift you up in prayer. If the busyness of life and parenting tasks prevent you from seeing with them face to face, you can still pray together over the phone.

There are some churches that have instituted a "Parent's Night Out," meaning that they provide free babysitting in order for parents to get a needed break. Perhaps this is something that you can institute in your church. Various parents can take turns each week and share in the childcare so all parents get their turn at a get-away evening.

The church and faith community can play a very supportive role in the parenting process. Here are a few additional ideas: Parenting Workshops/Seminars

· Family Retreats
· Church Lending Library
· Bible Study Groups on Parenting

PARTNERING WITH A PROFESSIONAL

Yes, there will be times when your mom, a friend, or a pastor may not be the best to go to in order to solve your situation. There are those times when professional help is needed. Why is it, however, that seeking professional counseling is something we often fail to do? Is there a stigma attached to it? When you or your child has a persistent high fever or an earache, we are quick to run to the physician. But we are not as quick

"No matter your particular parenting challenge, remember this, 'Prayer is the key to purpose-based parenting. It puts you in tune to divine wisdom to work out everything for good. So often parents don't pray because the outlook seems hopeless. But nothing is impossible with God. Nothing is so messed up that it cannot be fixed up, no relationship too strained for God to bring about reconciliation and understanding, no habit so deep-rooted that it cannot be up-rooted, no one is so weak that he cannot be strong, no child so willful that he cannot be obedient. Whatever your family needs trust God to supply it' " (Kuzma, 2006, p. 18).

to seek professional help if there are mental health issues. This is something that must be overcome.

When you became a parent, it came with your own past experiences and possible issues that affect the type of parent you are. Because there was probably no training before you became a parent, it is no wonder you may encounter challenges in which you need additional assistance. Parent counseling is a way for parents to understand why they do the things they do and gain a deeper understanding of themselves. Parent counseling is a great way to provide tools and techniques and give support to all parents that have issues around their role as a parent, and teach them things such as positive communication skills and conflict resolution.

LIST OF CHRISTIAN COUNSELORS
For a list of Adventist or other Christian counselors in your area, visit our Family Ministries website of the North American Division of Seventh-day Adventists at *http://www. adventistfamilyministries. com/article/70/resources/ directory-of-counselors*

Perhaps you could benefit from professional parent counseling if you:

· Have a child with a challenging temperament
· Feel that you need help disciplining your children
· Sometimes feel out of control or unsure of healthy ways to respond
· Want to better understand your child's behavior
· Want to learn about setting reasonable expectations and effective limits
· Want to increase your confidence and improve your parenting skills
  (Nemours Foundation, 2013)

There may also be times when you need to seek professional help for your child. Significant life events—such as the death of a family member, friend, or pet; divorce or a move; abuse; trauma; a parent leaving on military deployment; or a major illness in the family can cause stress that might lead to problems with behavior, mood, sleep, appetite, and academic or social functioning.

In some cases, it's not as clear what's caused a child to suddenly seem withdrawn, worried, stressed, sulky, or tearful. But if you feel your child might have an emotional or behavioral problem or needs help coping with a difficult life event, trust your instincts.

Here are some signs that your child may benefit from seeing a psychologist or licensed therapist:

· Developmental delay in speech, language, or toilet training
· Learning or attention problems (such as ADHD)
· Behavioral problems (such as excessive anger, acting out, bedwetting, or eating disorders)
· Episodes of sadness, tearfulness, or depression
· Social withdrawal or isolation
· Being the victim of bullying or bullying other children
· Decreased interest in previously enjoyed activities
· Overly aggressive behavior (such as biting, kicking, or hitting)
· Sudden changes in appetite

- Insomnia or increased sleepiness
- Mood swings (e.g., happy one minute, upset the next)
- Development of or an increase in physical complaints (such as headache, stomachache, or not feeling well) despite a normal physical exam by your doctor
- Management of a serious, acute, or chronic illness
- Problems in transitions (following separation, divorce, or relocation)
- Bereavement issues
- Custody evaluations
- Therapy following sexual, physical, or emotional abuse, or other traumatic events

(Nemours Foundation, 2013)

The bottom line is to trust your instincts as a parent. If you suspect that you or your child needs professional guidance, seek it immediately. The Family Ministries Department of the North American Division of Seventh-day Adventists has a database of Adventist and other Christian counselors to assist you as you seek professional help. You may go to our website at www.AdventistFamilyMinistries.com and click on the resource tab. There you will find a directory of Adventist counselors that are searchable by state and zip code. If there is no Adventist counselor in your area, you may also search for a Christian counselor. It is important that you seek biblically-based counseling. Remember, the decision is yours. This is only a tool to assist you in that decision. You will still need to call, check out the certifications, and decide if it is a good fit for your counseling needs.

WRAP UP
Never be afraid to seek help. Help may reveal itself in the form of a relative, a friend, a church member, or a professional. The important thing is to admit when you need help and to seek it. And no matter the situation, remember to always partner with God!

GROUP DISCUSSION

Discuss the statement below. How does it apply to parenting partners?

"At times the heart may be ready to faint; but a living sense of the dangers threatening the present and future happiness of their loved ones should lead Christian parents to seek more earnestly for help from the source of strength and wisdom" (White, 1954, p. 64).

GROUP ACTIVITY

As a group, list all of the resources that are available to parents in your community and in your church:

TRY THIS AT HOME
Here are some things to try at home this week:

1. Remember to continue the "Bible Promise Project" we started in chapter one. Find a promise in the Bible that you can apply to parent partnering. Write it out on an index card and put it in a prominent place in your home where you can see it throughout the day. Repeat it often, memorize it, and claim it as your own. And remember to share it the next time you meet with your group members.

2. Your child also needs to learn that it is OK to seek help when they need it. Talk to them about the types of things they may need help for and places or people they can go to for that help.

A PRAYER YOU MAY SAY
Dear Lord, open my eyes to see and understand your plan for my child. I will not be a stumbling block to your plans in my children's life. I want to be a good partner with You concerning my children's life. Father, have your way! In Jesus' name, Amen.

REFERENCES

Kids Count. (2005, July). "Parenting and family support." *Rhode Island Kids Count.* Providence, RI: Rhode Island. Retrieved from The Annie E. Casey Foundation, http://www.aecf.org/upload/publicationfiles/da3655k711.pdf

Kuzma, K, (2008) *The First 7 Years.* Pacific Press Publishing. Nampa, Idaho.

Nemours Foundation. (2013). *Kids Health.* Retrieved from: http://kidshealth.org/parent/positive/family/finding_therapist.html#

Thomas, G. (2005). *Devotions for Sacred Parenting.* Grand Rapids, MI: Zondervan.

White, E. G. (1954) *Child Guidance.* Hagerstown, MD: Review and Herald Publishing Association.

White, E. G. (1952). *The Adventist Home.* Hagerstown, MD: Review and Herald Publishing Association.

HELP! I'M A PARENT WEBSITE
Visit our parenting website to submit questions, find additional resources, follow a blog, sign up for a free parenting e-newsletter, and more: *www.HelpImAParent.org*

HELP! I'M A PARENT FACEBOOK PAGE
Like us on our Facebook page: "Help! I'm a Parent" New materials are posted on a regular basis.

Help! I'm a Parent: Christian Parenting in the Real World